Returnings: Poems of Love and Distance

RETURNINGS

POEMS OF LOVE AND DISTANCE

RAFAEL ALBERTI

Translated with an Introduction by
Carolyn L. Tipton

WHITE PINE PRESS / BUFFALO, NEW YORK

White Pine Press
P.O. Box 236 Buffalo, NY 14201
www.whitepine.org

Publication of this book was made possible, in part, by public funds from the New York State Council on the Arts, a State Agency; with funds from the National Endowment for the Arts, which believes that a great nation deserves great art; and with the support of the Amazon Literary Partnership.

Cover Art: Open Window, Collioure 1905, by Henri Matisse, © 2015 Succession H. Matisse / Artists Rights Society (ARS), New York

Printed and bound in the United States of America.

Library of Congress Control Number: 2015959245

ISBN: 978-1-935210-91-7

Acknowledgements

It is a pleasure to be able to thank all those who have helped with this project. I would first like to thank the National Endowment for the Arts, whose generous translation grant greatly facilitated my work. For help with the N.E.A.'s electronic application, I'd like to thank Jeff Ronner and Kit Dean. I would also like to thank the Banff Centre, where I was lucky enough to have four Leighton Studio Residencies over the course of several years. Many of Alberti's poems came to life in English while I translated in the Banff Centre's forest studios. There, also, I met Mercedes Gómez, whose explanations of some of Alberti's unusual constructions were very helpful.

To Rafael Alberti, himself, I am deeply grateful, and I thank him for having transmuted the suffering of his exile into this work of beauty, and for having extended his friendship to me.

I would especially like to thank Stephen Kessler, the Poetry Doctor, who gave detailed responses to all of my questions, clarified so many obscure portions of the Spanish texts, suggested possible interpretations, and helped to keep me focused on the whole rather than the particulars. For his unstinting and generous help and advice, and his inspiring example of excellence as a poet and translator, I can never thank him enough.

I'd also like to thank the American Literary Translators Association, many of whose talented members offered guidance and support. I'd particularly like to thank Lisa Bradford, Roger Greenwald, Susan Harris, Will Kirkland, and Marian Schwartz.

In addition, I'd like to thank Brian Bertino, Marta Maretich, Ann May, and James G. Tipton for their encouragement and interest; Shay Black, for the inspiration he has given me; Deianna Greet, Erica Pagels, and Paul Steuerwald for their help with the cover. Finally, I'd like to thank my dogs, Tristan and Olé, spiritual brothers of Alberti's Niebla, for their quiet companionship, and my husband, Frank Kucera, who buoyed me through difficulties, and enthusiastically greeted each new poem as it took shape.

A debt is also owed to earlier translators of some of the poems from Alberti's *Retornos*: Kenneth Rexroth, in particular, whose *Thirty Spanish Poems of Love and Exile*, Number Two in the City Lights Pocket Poet Series, contains six poems from *Retornos*, the first Alberti poems I ever read, and which have remained a continual source of pleasure and inspiration; Mark Strand, whose later anthology of Alberti's poems in his own translation, *The Owl's Insomnia*, includes seven beautiful translations from *Retornos*.

Grateful acknowledgment is made to the editors of the following periodicals in which these translations first appeared: *The Notre Dame Review*: "Returning on a Birthday (J.R.J.)," "Returning to a Blissful Island," "Love Returns on the Balcony," "Love Returns as It Once Was," "Love Returns on the Sands," "Love Returns at Night in the Woods." *Subtropics*: "Love Returns Up on the Roof." *Two Lines*: "Love Returns with the Moon."

—C.L.T.
Berkeley, 2016

TABLE OF CONTENTS

Part Two
RETORNOS DE AMOR
LOVE RETURNS

Part Three

Introduction

Carolyn L. Tipton

Rafael Alberti is considered to be one of Spain's greatest literary figures and one of the finest poets of the twentieth century. *Returnings* (*Retornos de lo vivo lejano*), written between 1948 and 1952, is one of his most beautiful books. Written while he was living in exile in Buenos Aires, these poems return to him a lost past. They are not just memories, but recreations in which the past comes alive again and becomes a living presence. Exile is temporarily transcended.

Alberti's life progressed in tandem with the Twentieth Century. Born in its infancy in 1902, in his youth he playfully experimented with many of the vanguard artistic movements of the 1920s—Cinematic Imagism, Cubism, Surrealism; during the social and political upheaval of the 1930s, he worked to bring about a more equitable society; later, he was plunged into war and then displacement and exile; finally, in his maturity, he reached an inner place of quiet from which he was able to begin to create again, but with a newly gained wisdom and perspective. The last is the period during which he wrote *Returnings*. Alberti continued to write throughout an exile that lasted almost forty years. Finally, invited back by the King of Spain, himself, Alberti returned home; he died in Spain in the waning days of the century, at the end of October 1999.

Early Poetic Influences

The earliest influences on his work were the Mediterranean Sea and the Prado Museum. Alberti was born on December 16, 1902, in Puerto de Santa María on the Bay of Cádiz, along whose shores he spent most of the hours of what he calls his "saltwork childhood." His poems are deeply imbued with his love of the sea, which he never lost despite his distance from it during much of his life. His family moved inland, to Madrid, the year Alberti turned fifteen. As far from the sea as he found himself, he thought he would never be happy again. Then he discovered the Prado Museum, which he called "the house of my adolescence." He set up an easel in front of the works of the Masters and taught himself to paint, becoming so proficient that he was invited to exhibit in Madrid's Autumn Salon in 1920. He developed a love of painting which was later reflected in the intensely imagistic quality of the

13

poems he would come to write. Throughout his time in Madrid, he was passionately devoted to the Prado. During the Civil War, he served as a director and as one of its guardians, working first to secure, and ultimately to move to safety, its many paintings. He speaks in "Returning to a Deserted Museum" of the haunting experience of walking around the emptied Prado. When he came to believe, in exile, that this world was forever lost to him, he wrote his tour-de-force *To Painting*, hoping to recreate the Prado's beauty and impact in words.

He might have remained focused on painting had it not been for two events: the death of his father in 1920 and his contraction of tuberculosis. His grief over his father's death was augmented by the almost simultaneous deaths of the famed matador Joselito and of the great Spanish novelist Benito Pérez Galdós. Alberti writes that his first poem was written beside his father's deathbed as an expression of his loss. It was at this time also that, convelescing from tuberculosis and forced to endure long periods of bedrest, he began to read avidly, and to write in the manner of the poets he was discovering, including both the classic poets, and the modern poets Antonio Machado and Juan Ramón Jiménez. He began to focus on his writing, and several of his early poems were published in avant-garde magazines. At the urging of a friend, he submitted his first book of poetry, a collection on a single theme, *Sailor on Land* (*Marinero en tierra*), to the Premio Nacional de Literatura, one of whose judges was Antonio Machado. In 1925, not yet twenty-three years old, his first book won Spain's national prize. This eventually drew him into the circle of poets who came to be known as the "Generation of '27." The group included Federico García Lorca, Luis Cernuda, Pedro Salinas, Jorge Guillén, and Vicente Aleixandre, among others. They gathered in the cafés of Madrid, where their rich exchanges about classical form, experimental techniques, and the purpose of poetry produced much creative ferment and many works, including Alberti's surrealist *Concerning the Angels* (*Sobre los ángeles, 1929*), ultimately bringing about a literary Renaissance there in the late 1920s.

The Second Spanish Republic

Also born during this period was the struggle against the dictator Primo de Rivera and a striving to create a new Spanish Republic. Alberti became politically engaged, reciting poems at demonstrations and tacking them up on walls. In 1931, a Republic was created and a little later, Alberti was given a grant by the new leadership to travel in Europe and report back on the contemporary art scene to a government eager to become part of the modern European community. He met many other artists on this trip, including Pablo Picasso, César Vallejo, Henri Michaux, Alejo Carpentier, Boris Pasternak, Maxim Gorky, Sergei Eisenstein, and Louis Aragon. He also, however, witnessed first-hand the rising menace of Fascism in Europe. He was present at the burning of the Reichstag. It was when remembering this trip that he later wrote "Return of a Sunset at Ravello," which voices the utopian hope he'd felt then that the increasingly imminent war would not come. Back at home, he rejoiced when the Popular Front—a coalition advocating land, educational, military, and economic reform—was voted into power in February, 1936.

At the same time that Alberti was being awakened politically, he was also undergoing another transformation. He met and became involved with the Spanish writer María Teresa León, who would become his wife and lifelong companion. Deeply in love, Alberti and León left for the Balearic island of Ibiza in July of 1936, expecting a romantic idyll.

The Spanish Civil War

However, on July 18, Franco's Fascists rose up against the Republic, initiating the Spanish Civil War. Ibiza came under Fascist control, detentions began, and Alberti and León were forced to flee into the mountains before ultimately making their escape back to the mainland. Alberti writes of the striking juxtaposition of the bliss of love and the fear of war in "Love Returns as a Fugitive in the Mountains": "The golden age of love had come, / but off the island, ships appeared."

Alberti was very active in the Republic's defense. Not only did he work to safeguard the paintings in the Prado, he also served as Secretary of the Alliance of Antifascist Intellectuals. He organized the Second International Congress of Writers to help publicize Spain's predicament, traveling to Paris and Moscow to invite the delegates, including Stephen Spender, André Malraux, Langston Hughes, Nicolás Guillén, and Octavio Paz; he published a magazine in which most of the important writing of the time reached the front; he presented short theatrical pieces ("theater of urgency") and recited poems—composed specifically for them—to troops at the front whenever there were pauses in the fighting.

Unfortunately, with the massive aid of men and matériel from Hitler and Mussolini, unchecked by the U.S., England, or France, who refused to help, the Spanish Fascist forces were crushing the Republicans. By March of 1939, Spain had fallen to Franco. Lorca had been murdered by Fascists in Granada, Antonio Machado had died in a refugee camp in France, and Miguel Hernández had been imprisoned; most of the survivors of Alberti's generation had already left Spain, and now Alberti and his wife fled for their lives, making a miraculous escape on a single-engine plane to Orán, Algeria, and thence to Paris twenty-four hours before Franco entered Madrid. Within months, World War II had begun, the Pétain government withdrew their work and residence permits, and they found themselves facing the threat of German troops. Forced to flee again, they escaped Europe on a boat bound from Marseilles to Buenos Aires, where they were warmly welcomed and decided to settle.

The Years of Exile

The Spanish Civil War changed Alberti's life forever. He now began an exile that was to last nearly four decades. Alberti's first book of this period was *Between the Carnation and the Sword* (*Entre el clavel y la espada*, 1939–40), a title which perfectly describes his existential state, torn between his anger and sorrow over the loss of Spain, and his hope for renewal and desire to create beauty once again. Gradually, he began a new life. A daughter was born to him. His bitterness became tempered, and he entered a period of creative expansion.

16

He wrote plays and collaborated in compositions and performances with musicians; he also began to work with visual artists and once more started to paint.

It was now—in the late 1940s and early 1950s—that he produced the two great works of his high maturity, *To Painting* (*A la pintura*, 1945–48) and *Returnings*. Like *To Painting*, *Returnings* is born of his exile, but it is *Returnings* in which exile is, itself, the subject. It is here that he communicates most clearly his experience of exile. In Alberti's earlier poetry, he had so often looked back—with nostalgia for the sea in *Sailor on Land*, with a sense of paradise lost in *Concerning the Angels*—but in *Returnings*, he is writing in literal exile, and this reification of an emotional state he'd so often gravitated towards intensifies the feeling of exile evoked here.

RETURN TO EUROPE

In 1963, Alberti uprooted himself once again. Compelled by the worsening political situation there, Alberti left Argentina and moved to Italy, home of his paternal grandparents. Finally, in 1977, after the death of Franco, Alberti was able to return home to Spain after an exile of almost forty years. During his last years in Argentina and his stay in Italy, Alberti had become more and more of a public figure, speaking at conferences, exhibiting his paintings, and especially, giving readings of his poetry. This activity increased when he returned to Spain, where he found that, in the years following the Spanish diaspora, he had become, for many, a symbol of survival, of resistance, of the unquenchable flame of the artistic spirit. He actively entered into Spanish political and cultural life, even serving briefly in the Spanish Cortes (parliament). On his eightieth birthday, he gave a poetry reading which had to be held in Madrid's bullring, so great was the crowd who wanted to hear him.

In his last few decades, Alberti was awarded many prizes and honors, including the Premio Cervantes, currently Spain's most prestigious literary prize, honoring a lifetime of literary achievement. Alberti ultimately published some twenty-four volumes of poetry, produced over seven decades, as well as several plays, some non-fiction prose, and a five-volume autobiography,

The Lost Grove. Late in his life, a widower, he married the scholar María Asunción Mateo, and with her he moved back to Puerto de Santa María, where he spent his final years, realizing, he said, by his return to his native village, "all the dreams of my exile."

RETURNINGS: POEMS OF LOVE AND DISTANCE

Returnings is a book of luminous evocations of people and places from the poet's lost country. For many Spanish readers, *Returnings* is their favorite work by Alberti. For the poet, too, *Returnings* always held a special place. Here, it's not only that, through acts of poetic imagination, he returns to his past but also that his past actively returns to *him*. He spoke about the experience of writing this book:

> "In those years of Argentinian exile, my distant Spanish life would present itself to me down to the minutest details; the memories—places, people, desires, loves, sorrows, joys—would invade me hour by hour, making of my poem not an elegy for things that were dead, but, on the contrary, a living presence, come back [to me] of the things in this world that do not die but go on existing, even in spite of their apparent distance. [It was a] book without end, then, like a chronicle of the best and worst moments of my life, of those for whose return I would always hope."[1]

Alberti's poems of these moments are presented to us in a particular way. Like *To Painting* and the great works of his youth, *Sailor on Land* and *Concerning the Angels*, *Returnings* has been structured with great care, this time into three parts. The first, untitled, part includes poems in which memories of the poet's childhood, youth, and early adulthood return to him; the second, titled "Love Returns," is a section of love poems in which he mainly recalls the early days of his love affair with his first wife, María Teresa León; in the third part, untitled like the first, it is the places, friends, and emotions of his more recent past that return to him. A slightly different take on how to look at these parts is suggested by Jaime Siles, the editor of Alberti's collected poetry: "The first part is centered in the 'I,'" he says, "the second, in the 'you,' and the third, in 'the other.'"[2] So, in Part One, the poet is directed inward, describing what shaped him; in Part Two, he is directed solely toward his beloved; in Part Three, he is directed outward, toward the world at large, particularly Spain.

Then, there is a further structuring. The poems in each section appear in loose chronological order. Part One begins with poems about his childhood, and progresses through poems about his youth, including the time of the war. Part Two begins with a poem that recounts his first sight of María Teresa ("Love Returns As It First Appeared") and ends with a "memory" of a time that has not happened yet ("Love Returns to a Place It's Never Been"). Part Three begins with a memory of Europe just before the war ("Return of a Sunset at Ravello") and proceeds to the more recent years of his exile, including his first poignant view of Spain in many years, seen distantly from on board a ship bound for another country ("Return of the Spanish Coastline").

Even the individual lines of the poems reflect Alberti's desire to create order in his work, contributing, he hoped, in his own small way, to a greater harmony in the world around him. This was his ideal in his art. Of *To Painting*, Alberti said that it was fashioned "after all the chaos" and set up in opposition to it. In *Returnings*, his desire for order and harmony is partly manifested by his use of a guiding meter: Alberti has composed most of the poems using the classic Spanish *alejandrino*, a fourteen-syllable line. I have tried to imitate his formal music by giving my translated lines the underpinnings of English poetry's own classical line, the iambic pentameter. The sonorous, resonant quality of Alberti's verse underlines his elegaic tone with its blend of praise and lament. The poems greatly benefit from being read aloud.

This translation's source is the edition of *Returnings* found in Losada's 1961 publication of Alberti's *Poesías completas*, generally agreed to be the definitive edition of *Returnings*. Alberti first published *Returnings* in 1952, but following his usual practice with his books of poetry, he continued to add and subtract poems from the original collection. In the years that followed the first pub-

19

lication of *Returnings*, he not only added three poems to Part Three, but he more than doubled Part Two, which had originally contained eight poems and now contained twenty. Some of the poems added to Part Two further augment what Spanish critic Torres Nebrera calls the "Ibiza Suite," the group of poems—not all found together—in which Alberti remembers his days on Ibiza in the summer of 1936, in which passion and terror were so jarringly juxtaposed. Part Two is the section of which Alberti was clearly most fond. These are the poems so many of his Spanish readers know by heart, drawn to them not just for their beauty, excitement, and tenderness, but also because it is here, more than in other parts of the book, that memories not only return but come alive. These twenty poems, found at the center of the book, are truly the heart of *Returnings*.

To draw attention to this for the English reader, I have taken the translational liberty of incorporating this notion into the title, changing *Retornos de lo vivo lejano* (literally, *Returns of What Is Alive [and] Distant*) to *Returnings: Poems of Love and Distance*. Another liberty I have taken involves my choice of poems. Following Alberti's own practice of tinkering with his original structure, I have subtracted a few poems. With the exception of one poem from Part One, all the subtractions were made from Part Three. A single poem was taken out because, like the excepted poem in Part One, it didn't work well in English, but the rest were left out because they do not fit with the book's theme of nostalgia for his past in Spain. Two of these were poems Alberti wrote about Argentina's dictator, Perón, and the other three were all later additions he had tacked on to the end of the section, dedicated to writer friends, two of whom weren't even Spanish.

Until now, *Returnings* has never appeared as a whole in English, although isolated poems from the book have continued to appear in anthologies of Alberti's work in translation throughout the decades since its publication. Many poets, including Kenneth Rexroth, Ben Belitt, and Mark Strand, have each translated a few poems from *Returnings*. What explains this continued appeal? A longing for the past is, of course, a deep-running current in human nature. Moreover, especially now, in this present alienating age of electronic ubiquity, regressive politics, and a rapidly disappearing natural world, many of us have

begun to feel that we, too, exist in a kind of exile. But it is not just our iden-
tification with Alberti's longing and his sense of exile that causes us to con-
tinue to embrace *Returnings*, but also the delight readers share with him when
he succeeds at truly re-experiencing what had been lost. We feel that we, too,
have won when melancholy elegy temporarily gives way to gladness. Now
that the poems in *Returnings* are appearing all together here in English for the
first time, more readers, I hope, will finally be able to experience what Al-
berti's art was able to shape from his exile. I wish readers joy in their discovery
of Alberti's vivid evocations of his lost, and re-found, world.

[1]. From an interview in Rome in 1974. Quoted by Barbara Dale May in *El dilema de la nostalgia
en la poesía de Alberti*. Utah Studies in Literature and Linguistics. Las Vegas: Peter Lang, 1978.
[2] From Jaime Siles' commentary in *Rafael Alberti: Obras completas: Poesía III*. Edicíon de Jaime
Siles. Barcelona: Editorial Seix Barral, 2006.

Part One

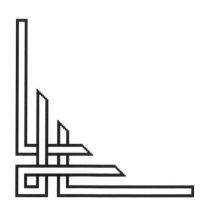

RETORNOS DE UNA TARDE DE LLUVIA

También estará ahora lloviendo, neblinando
en aquellas bahías de mis muertes,
de mis años aún vivos sin muertes.
También por la neblina entre el pinar, lloviendo,
lloviendo, y la tormenta también, los ya distantes
truenos con gritos celebrados, últimos,
el fustazo final del rayo por las torres.
Te asomarías tú, vejez blanca, saliéndote
de tus templadas sábanas de nietos y ojos dulces,
y mi madre a los vidrios de colores
del alto mirador que descorría
una ciudad azul de níveas sombras
con barandales verdes
resonados de súbito a la tarde
por los dedos que el mar secretamente
y como por descuido abandona en la brisa.

Saldría yo con Agustín, con José Ignacio
y con Paquillo, el hijo del cochero,
a buscar caracoles por las tapias
y entre los jaramagos de las tumbas,
o por la enretamada arboleda perdida
a lidiar becerrillos todavía con sustos
de alegres colegiales sorprendidos de pronto.
(Estas perdidas ráfagas que vuelven sin aviso,
estas precipitadas palabras de los bosques,
diálogo interrumpido, confidencias

RETURNING ON A RAINY EVENING

It must also be raining now, misting,
on that Bay of my dead, of those years
still alive to me, untouched by death.
Raining, too, through the mists of the pine grove,
raining and storming, there, too, the celebrative
shouts of thunder moving off now, and last,
the final flash of lightning by the towers.
Now the old one would reappear, leaving a bed
warmed by little children with sweet eyes,
and my mother, on the stained-glass balcony
looking out on a city
blue with clear-cut shadows,
with green balustrades
echoed in the evening by thin fingers of foam
which the sea in secret, pretending
carelessness, abandons to the breeze.

I'd go out with Agustín, with José Ignacio
and the coachman's son, Paquillo,
to search for snails along the walls
or under wild mustard flowers on the graves,
or we'd go across the lost grove, thick with broom,
to bullfight the young calves, who still
could scare us when they took us by surprise.
(Lost tag-ends of the storm burst out of nowhere,
trees fling out words, conversations
break off, the sea

del mar y las arenas empapadas.)
Reclino la cabeza,
llevo el oído al hoyo de la mano
para pasar mejor lo que de lejos
con las olas de allí, con las de allá,
chorreando, me viene. Oigo un galope
fatigando la orilla de castillos,
de bañadas ruinas y escaleras
con los pies destrozados en el agua.

Yo sé quién va, yo sé quién se desboca
cantando en ese potro negro de sal y espuma.
¿Adónde corre, adónde,
hacia qué submarinas puertas, hacia qué umbrales
de azul movido, hacia qué adentros claros,
en busca de un perfil, una compacta
forma, línea, color, relieve, música,
tangible, definida?
Quiere los arcos, busca los dinteles
que dan a los difíciles poblados sin neblinas,
armónicas comarcas, firmamentos precisos,
cielos sin nebulosas,
paraísos sin humo.

Llueve sin mar, sin mar, sin mar. Borrada
la mar ha sido por la bruma. Pronto
se llevará los bosques también, y ni estos troncos
tan posibles, tan fáciles,
cimbrearán de pie para decirme
que han muerto, que se han muerto

whispers its soaked secrets to the sands.)
I tilt my head, cup my hand
to my ear, and listening
to the waves crashing far off
and the wash rushing to shore,
I strain for what the sea is telling me.
I hear galloping, it's wearing down
the castle walls, the drenched ruins, the crumbling
staircase leading down into the water.

I know who's galloping, riding wild, singing
on that black colt of salt and spume.
Where is he running to, where,
towards what underwater portal, what lintel
of shifting blues, what bright interior,
in search of a lost profile, a palpable
form, a line, a color, a sharp
outline, tangible and definite.
He's looking for the archway or the door
that opens onto cities without mist,
harmonious spaces, firmaments
clearly vaulted, cloudless skies,
paradises without smoke.

Rain and rain, and no more sea. No sea. The sea
has disappeared inside the fog. Soon,
the forest, too, will be erased
—it will happen easily—not even
these trunks will sway towards me
to tell me they have died, that on this night

esta tarde de nieblas y de lluvia mis ojos.
¿Quién ve en lo oscuro,
quién pretende sombras,
quién concretar la noche sin estrellas?
Se murió el mar, se murió el mar, murieron
con él las cosas que llegaron. Quedan,
ya sólo quedan, ¿oyes?
una conversación confusa, un errabundo
coloquio sin palabras que entender, un temido,
un invasor espanto
a regresar sin ojos, a cerrarlos sin sueño.

of rain and fog, my eyes are dying too.
Who can see in this thick dark, who
can take on these deep shadows, give
solidity and form to the starless night?
The sea is dead, the sea is dead, and with it
everything that's had its day.
All that remains—can you hear?—
a jumbled conversation, a speech
that has somehow lost its words,
a creeping dread. Have I come back to this:
open my eyes, and I can't see; close them, I can't sleep.

RETORNOS DE LOS DÍAS COLEGIALES

Por jazmines caídos recientes y corolas
de dondiegos de noche vencidas por el día,
me escapo esta mañana inaugural de octubre
hacia los lejanísimos años de mi colegio.

¿Quién eres tú, pequeña sombra que ni proyectas
el contorno de un niño casi a la madrugada?
¿Quién, con sueño enredado todavía en los ojos,
por los puentes del río vecino al mar, andando?
Va repitiendo nombres a ciegas, va torciendo
de memoria y sin gana las esquinas. No ignora
que irremediablemente la calle de la Luna,
la de las Neverías, la del Sol y las Cruces
van a dar al cansancio de algún libro de texto.

¿Qué le canta la cumbre de la sola pirámide,
qué la circunferencia que se aburre en la página?
Afuera están los libres araucarios agudos
y la plaza de toros
con su redonda arena mirándose en el cielo.

Como un látigo, el 1 lo sube en el pescante
del coche que el domingo lo lleva a las salinas
y se le fuga el 0 rodando a las bodegas,
aro de los profundos barriles en penumbra.

El mar reproducido que se expande en el muro
con las delineadas islas en breve rosa,

RETURNING TO SCHOOL DAYS

Through fallen jasmine and corollas
of night-blooming dondiegos crushed by light,
I escape on this first morning of October
to my faraway school days.

Who are you, small shadow that can scarcely cast
a boy's outline in early morning light?
Who, with the scenes of dreams still in his eyes,
runs on the river-bridge close to the sea?
He runs repeating names, without seeing, turning corners
from memory, but without desire. He knows
that irremediably, the Avenue of the Moon,
the Avenues of the Ice-Seller, the Sun, and the Crosses
will lead right to the boredom of some textbook.

What can the pyramid's height sing to him,
or the circumference that wearies the whole page?
Outside are the Araucaria pines, sharp-scented, free,
and the bull-ring
with its round arena gazing at the sky.

I looks like the coachman's whip, carried
to the salt-marshes each Sunday.
0 escapes too, rolling to the wine-cellars,
a new hoop for the barrels down in shadow.

The simulated sea spread on the wall
—islands marked by tiny points of rose—

no adivina que el mar verdadero golpea
con su aldabón azul los patios del recreo.

¿Quién es este del cetro en la lámina muerta,
o aquel que en la lección ha perdido el caballo?
No está lejos el río que la sombra del rey
melancólicamente se llevó desmontada.

Las horas prisioneras en un duro pupitre
lo amarran como un pobre remero castigado
que entre las paralelas rejas de los renglones
mira su barca y llora por asirse del aire.

Estas cosas me trajo la mañana de octubre,
entre rojos dondiegos de corolas vencidas
y jazmines caídos.

can't guess that the real sea
is pounding its blue knocker on the playground.

Who is this with a sceptre in the print?
Which guy in the lesson lost his horse?
We're not far from the river where the ghost
of the dismounted king fled off in grief.

Captive hours bind him to his desk
like a poor galley slave who, between the lines
of benches, glimpses his own boat
and cries to be out in the open air.

This morning all these things come back to me
through dondiegos, their scarlet dimmed by day,
and jasmine fallen away.

RETORNOS DE UNA MAÑANA DE PRIMAVERA

Quizás con igual número, con la misma incontable
numeración de olas que desde el nacimiento
de tu divina espalda azul has conmovido,
me llamas resonando,
reventando tu frente de espumas en la orilla
donde mi luminoso corazón miró siempre,
mar mío, sobre ti soplar la primavera.

Desde tantas angustias sin eco, desde tantos
días iguales, noches de un mismo rostro, desde
las similares cuevas de cada hora, es dulce
no ofrecer resistencia a tu verde llamada.

¿Qué me abres, qué rotos
puros y antiguos arcos blanquísimos? ¿Qué esbeltas
columnatas tranquilas, finos fustes tronchados,
qué playeros castillos sin nadie me levantas?
Ausentes de rumores callan las brisas, muda
la arena de los ágiles pies está, y silenciosos
de la desnuda siesta del amor los pinares.
Deja a mi corazón llenarlos de alegría.

Desciende, niña mía, de las torres. Tú eres
mi hermana, sí, mi hermana. La más pequeña. Vamos,
descalzos por las rocas, en los presos olvidos
del agua, en sus dorsales
osamentas, sin miedo
contra los insufribles moluscos obstinados.

RETURNING ON A SPRING MORNING

With the same uncountable number of waves
—wave upon wave—you've continually raised
from the time of your blue birth,
you call me now, resounding,
breaking your foamy brow against the shore
where my luminous heart always watched you,
lovely sea, stirred up by the Spring breeze.

After so much monotonous pain, after
so many days and nights each wearing the same face,
after the identical dark cave of every hour,
it's so sweet just to yield to your green call.

What will your waves open now? What
broken, pure white arches, what slender
colonnades and delicate split shafts, what
sandcastles will you have shaped to show me?
With no voices to blend with, the breeze has gone quiet,
the track is without flying feet, and the pinegrove
is silent, lacking Love's naked siestas.
Let my heart's noisy joy fill them up.

Come down now from the tower, little one:
my sister! The youngest of us all. Let's go
barefooted on the rocks, beside the sea's
forgetful prison—look, half-buried
dorsal skeletons—nor will we fear
the sticky, stubborn mollusks.

Persígueme en las libres afueras de las olas.
Es la edad en que el viento sueña en doblar al viento.
Llévame, ciegamente victoriosa, ceñida
tu cabeza de algas, hacia los ondulados
linderos que aureolan los blancos retamares.

¿Quién no puede, escondido,
desde los trasparentes alertas en las dunas,
mirar, hermana mía, las cosas que otros ojos
por oscuros no vieron?

¿Quién me veda poblarte, hoy a tanta distancia,
las playas de aquel día, de aquel largo poniente,
con el recién subido potro del mar llevando
la primavera alzada en su borrén de espumas?

Mucho has llorado, hermana, para que yo no pueda
llenarte las orillas de pasos venturosos,
de columpiadas flores la rota arquitectura
y de un amor las copas jubilosas del aire.

Recibe lo que el mar me trajo esta mañana
y suplícale siempre para mi sus retornos.

Chase me to the outskirts of the waves.
Here, the wind dreams of bending to the wind.
Now race me blindly back, victorious, your head
circled with seaweed, past the evermoving
edges haloing the heathered scrubland.

Hidden in the dunes, so alert that the world
became transparent, how could we not,
little sister, gaze out on things that others,
in their darkness, couldn't see?

Who can stop me from returning—now, from so far—
to the beaches of that day, the long sunset,
the new-risen colt of the sea, bearing high
in its saddle of foam, all of Spring.

Little sister, you've long wept, for I'm not there
to fill the sands with lucky footprints, or
the broken architecture of the waves with flowers,
or with love, the jubilant and singing cups of air.

Take what the sea has brought to me this morning,
and beg it to let me always keep returning.

RETORNOS DE CHOPIN A TRAVÉS DE UNAS MANOS YA IDAS

A mi madre,
que nos unía a todos en la
música de su viejo piano.

Era en el comedor, primero era en el dulce
comedor de los seis: Agustín y María,
Milagritos, Vicente, Rafael y Josefa.
De allí me viene ahora, invierno aquí, distantes,
casi perdidos ya, desvanecidos míos,
hermanos que no pude llevar a mi estatura;
de allí me viene ahora este acorde de agua,
de allí también, ahora,
esta nocturna rama de arboleda movida,
esta orilla de mar, este amor, esta pena
que hoy, velados en lágrimas, me juntan a vosotros
a través de unas manos dichosas que se fueron.

Era, luego, en la sala del rincón en penumbra,
lejos del comedor primero de los seis,
y aunque cerca también de vosotros, perdido,
casi infinitamente perdido me sentíais,
muy tarde, ya muy tarde,
cuando empieza a agrandarse la llegada del sueño,
un acorde de agua, una rama nocturna,
una orilla, un amor, una pena a vosotros
dulcemente me unían
a través de unas manos cansadas que se fueron.

Y es ahora, distante,
más infinitamente que entonces, desterrado

RETURNING TO CHOPIN,
BROUGHT TO LIFE BY HANDS NOW GONE

> For my mother,
> who joined us together
> through the music of her old piano

It was in the dining room first, in that sweet
room where the six of us would gather: Agustín and María,
Milagritos, Vicente, Rafael and Josefa.
From there this music comes to me—winter here,
my brothers and sisters, who never rose to join me,
so distant now and almost lost to me;
from there this music comes to me,
this chord of water,
this nocturne, a bough stirring in a grove,
a shore beside the sea, this love and grief
that today, deepened by tears, join me to you all
through joyful hands that vanished.

It happened later in the shadowed corner room,
far from the children's dining room;
although we all sat close
you felt so far away from me
that it was long and late
before the dream finally arrived:
a chord of water, a nocturne-bough,
a shore beside the sea, the love and grief
by which we all were sweetly joined
through wearied hands that vanished.

And now once more, with the distance between us
so much greater than before. Exiled

del comedor primero, del rincón en penumbra
de la sala, es ahora,
cuando aquí, tembloroso,
traspasado de invierno el corazón, María,
Vicente, Milagritos, Agustín, y Josefa,
uno, el seis, Rafael, vuelve a unirse a vosotros,
por la rama, el amor, por el mar y la pena,
a través de unas manos lloradas que se fueron.

from the first dining room, as well as
the shadowed corner room, trembling,
his heart pierced through
by winter, O María,
Vicente, Milagritos, Agustín, Josefa,
one of us, the sixth one, Rafael, rejoins you now
with the arrival of our bough, our love, our sea, our grief
through much-missed hands that vanished.

RETORNOS DE UN DÍA DE CUMPLEAÑOS (J.R.J.)

Subí yo aquella tarde
con mis primeros versos
a la sola azotea
donde entre madreselvas y jazmines
él en silencio ardía.
Le llevaba yo estrofas
de mar y marineros,
médanos amarillos,
añil claro de sombras
y muros de cal fresca
estampados de fuentes y jardines.
Le llevaba también
tardes de su colegio,
horas tristes de estudio,
mapas coloreados,
azul niño de atlas,
pizarras melancólicas,
blancas del sufrimiento de los números.
Subía yo este ramo
de naturales, tiernas,
alegres, breves cosas sucedidas,
con el mismo temblor
de árbol sobrecogido
que en un día de fiesta
me cubrió cuando quise
llegar al pararrayos de la torre.
Estaba él derramado
como cera encendida en el crepúsculo,

RETURNING ON A BIRTHDAY (J.R.J.)*

I climbed up that afternoon
with my first poems
to the solitary rooftop
where he glowed amidst the silence
of jasmine & honeysuckle.
I brought him stanzas
about the sea & sailors,
yellow dunes,
the indigo of shadows on wet sand,
and whitewashed walls of lime
with silhouettes of fountains & of gardens.
I also brought
our schoolday afternoons,
sad hours spent in studying,
colored maps,
the childhood blue of atlases,
and melancholy blackboards,
white with the suffering of numbers.
I climbed out on this bough
of everyday, sweet,
brief-lived, bright, past things,
with the same trembling
as when, on a fiesta day, concealed
by an astonished tree,
I tried to reach
the tower's lightning rod.
He was lavish
as a candle burned at dusk,

sobre el pretil abierto
a los montes con nieve perdonada
por la morena mano
de junio que venía.
Hablamos con vehemencia
de nuestro mar, lo mismo
que del amigo ausente
a quien se está queriendo
ver de un momento a otro
después de muchos años.
Cuando se entró la noche
y apenas le veía,
era su opaca voz,
era tal vez la sombra
de su voz la que hablaba
todavía del mar,
del mar como si acaso
no fuera a llegar nunca.
¡Oh señalado tiempo!
Él entonces tenía
la misma edad que hoy,
dieciséis de diciembre,
tengo yo aquí, tan lejos
de aquella tarde pura
en que le subí el mar
 a su sola azotea.

leaning on a railing open
to the mountains, their snow
still spared by the brown hand
of early June.
We spoke with vehemence
about our sea, the same
as of an absent friend
whom one expects
to see at any moment
after many years.
When night flowed in
and I could hardly see him,
he became just his dark voice,
or, perhaps, the shadow
of his voice which still
spoke of the sea,
of the sea, as if he might not,
after all, reach it again.
How striking to think
he was then
the same age I am today,
the sixteenth of December,
so far from that
pure afternoon on which
I climbed up to his solitary rooftop
bringing the sea.

*the poet Juan Ramón Jiménez

RETORNOS DE UN DÍA DE RETORNOS

Algún día quizás, seguramente, alguien
(alguien a quien siquiera pueda ofrecer tal nombre)
se acordará de mí pensándome tan lejos
y dirá lo que yo, si hubiese retornado.

Aquí estás, ya has venido, con más noche en la frente.
Llegas de caminante, de romero a tu patria.
Los lugares que hiciste, las horas que creaste,
pasados todavía de tu luz y tu sombra,
salen a recibirte.

¿Qué tienes?, te pregunta primero la azotea
desde la que miraste tantas veces morirse
con la noche las piedras del Escorial, las cumbres
rodadas de otros nombres,
otras nieves y ocultas ramas que te habitaron.

Algo quisieras tú decirte al verte, pero
sabes bien que el arroyo
que corre por tu voz nunca ha de repetirse,
que a tu imagen pasada no altera la presente.

Entra, sé el visitante de tus propias alcobas,
el viajero lejano de tus mismos salones,
el huésped melancólico, errabundo en tu casa.
Éstos son tus amigos junto a la chimenea.
Tú no faltas en medio con un libro en la mano.
Te escuchan. En los ojos
de algunos ya es su muerte la que te está atendiendo.

RETURNING ON A DAY IT'S ALL RETURNED

Some day surely someone
(someone I can't even name)
remembering me so far away
will imagine me returning.

Here you are. With more night in your face.
You've come home as a stranger.
The places that you made, the hours you created—
still striped by your shadow, by your light—
stir to greet you.

What's wrong? the rooftop asks. You go there first,
having watched so many times as light died
on the stones of El Escorial, the peaks
covered now by other names, other snows,
and secret paths whose map once lived in you.

When you see yourself, you want to say something,
but you know that the stream flowing on with your voice
can't repeat itself, that your image from the past
can't be altered by you now.

Walk in. You're a visitor now, a traveler
from a place far from these rooms, a melancholy
guest, wandering in your own house.
There are your friends by the fire, and you
in the middle, reading aloud. They're listening to you
then, but in the eyes of some, you can see now
death's already there and staring back at you.

Mira tu lecho. Es ése.
Dormido, en él estás, en él, aunque no hay nadie,
aunque de la almohada se haya escapado el sueño.
Todavía un vestido sin esperanza espera
llenarse de tus pulsos para seguir andando.

Asómate un instante. Tus alegres cocinas
aún guardan el rescoldo de aquel último fuego.
Los platos te contemplan desde los anaqueles
y en el vasar los finos cristales de colores.
Contra el muro, aclarada,
flauta azul, se desvive
la minúscula sombra del precioso canario.

Al dejar el vestíbulo,
ya no tienes más ámbito que el de los escalones
que uno a uno descienden a las viejas aceras,
ni más dulce consuelo que perderte invisible,
peregrino en tu patria, por sus vivos retornos.

Look at your bed. You slept in it so often
it's almost as if you're there, even though there's
no one, and all your dreams have long escaped the pillow.
A suit still waits without much hope
to be filled again and walk out in the world.

Peek in here: your cozy cooking stove
still holds the ashes of that final fire.
The dishes contemplate you from the shelves,
the delicate colored crystal.
Against the wall, small bright blue flute,
the tiny shadow of your precious canary
calls out.

Back at the door, there's no place left to go
but the stairs, which one by one descend
to the old sidewalk, nor any sweeter consolation
than to have walked invisibly through your old place
through the grace of this vivid return.

RETORNOS DE UNA ISLA DICHOSA

La felicidad vuelve con el nombre ligero
de un presuroso y grácil joven alado: Aire.
Por parasoles verdes, las sombras que retornan
contestan, y el amor, por otro nombre: Isla.

Venid, días dichosos, que regresáis de lejos
teniendo por morada las velas de un molino;
por espejo de luna, la que el sol tiró al pozo,
y por bienes del alma,
todo el mar apresado en pequeñas bahías.

Llegad, alegres olas de mis años, risueños
labios de espuma abierta de las blancas edades.
Suenen mis ojos, canten con repetidas lágrimas
al pastor que desnudo da a la mar sus ovejas.

Ven otra vez, doblada
maravilla incansable de los viejos olivos.
Me abracen nuevamente tus raíces, hundiéndome
en las tumbas que muestran su soledad al cielo.

Quiero tocaros, santas, invencibles higueras,
abatidas de zumos, pero no de cansancio.
Dejadme en la apretada oscuridad inmóvil
de vuestra fresca alcoba dormir tranquilamente.

Soñar, soñar dormido, desde allí, en las colinas
donde los algarrobos

RETURNING TO A BLISSFUL ISLAND

Happiness comes back with the light name
of a quick and graceful fluttering of wings: Air.
Beneath the parasol pines, love in a green shade
answers by another name: Island.

Come blissful days, returning from so far,
having for a home the windmill's sails;
for mirror, what the sun flung in the well,
and for the soul's wealth,
all the sea, caught and held in little bays.

Arrive, blithe waves of those days, smiling
lips of foam opening through the white ages.
Let my eyes sing tears for the shepherd of the sea,
repeatedly bereft of all his sheep.

Come back to me, bent marvels,
old, unwearied olive trees, whose roots
plunge down beneath the graves
where loneliness lies open to the sky.

I want to touch you, sacred fig trees,
all out of juice but not fatigue, and yet
unbeaten. Let me sleep peacefully
in the cool bedroom made by your shade.

And to dream, having fallen asleep in those hills
where the carob trees add honey

dan su miel a las nieves de la flor del almendro;
desde donde calladas huertas corren sus límites
abriendo arcos de cal arrobados de adelfas.

Despierte, al descorrer las ramas, ya en la tarde,
padeciendo el deseo de morirme en las dunas,
cuando al sol no le espera más final que el antiguo
de embozarse en los hombros mojados de la noche.

Isla de amor, escúchame, antes de que te vayas,
antes, ya que has venido, de que escapes de nuevo:
Concédeme la gracia de aclarar los perfiles
del canto que a mi lengua le quede aún, poniéndole
esa azul y afilada delgadez de contornos
que subes cuando al alba renaces sin rubores,
feliz y enteramente desnuda, de las olas.

to the snow of all the almond trees in bloom;
where orchards, grown quiet, overrun their bounds
past opening arches rapturous with rose-bay.

Then to waken, part the boughs, find it evening now,
and wish to die in the dunes like the sun—
nothing final in its ancient ritual:
snuffed by the wet shoulders of the night.

Island of love, listen to me—now
that you've come—before you slip away again:
Grant me the grace to make clear the shape
of the song still on my tongue, giving it
the same slender blue contour
you raise at dawn when, blissful and perfectly
nude, you're reborn from the waves.

RETORNOS A TRAVÉS DE LOS COLORES

Esta tarde te alivian los colores: el verde,
aparecido niño grácil de primavera,
el claro mar del cielo que cambia en los cristales
el ala sonreída de un añil mensajero.

Te hacen viajar el blanco tembloroso y erguido
que abren las margaritas contra la enredadera,
el marfil de los senos nacientes del magnolio,
el albo de las calas de pie sobre el estanque.

Piensas en los colores lejanos de otros días:
aquel azul dormido de espalda en los esteros,
el áureo de las piedras derribadas al borde
de los dientes antiguos de su mar endiosado.

Escuchas en el rosa del rosal el caído
de los lazos tronchados tras el balcón del arpa,
y en el negro fulgente de las sombras, el lustre
del sombrero difunto de los altos abuelos.

No pierdas los colores que te juegan caminos
esta tarde en tu breve jardín murado. Mira.
Aquí están. Tú los tocas. Son los mismos colores
que en tu corazón viven ya un poco despintados.

RETURNING THROUGH COLOR

This afternoon, the colors here console you: green
has arrived, Spring's graceful child; the sky's
clear sea, seen in the glass, casts
blue on the homing pigeon's smiling wing.

Whites take you back: the tremulous and upright white
the daisies raise to face the twining vines,
the ivory of the magnolia's budding breasts,
the snow white of the lilies on the pond.

You think of the distant colors of those days:
blue sleeping on its back across the bay,
the gold of pebbles scattered on the shore
amidst the ancient teeth of godly seas.

In the roses' pink, you hear the trellis fall:
petals on the harp-strings of the balcony;
and in the shadows' burnished black, the luster
of tall grandfathers' dead hats.

Don't miss out on the colors that open paths for you
this afternoon in your small garden. Look.
Here they are. You touch them: they're the same
as the colors that live in your heart, a little faded now.

RETORNOS DE UN MUSEO DESHABITADO

Algo me queda siempre cuando estoy solo, cuando
emprendiendo el camino del corazón, subiendo
las empinadas cuestas de la memoria, elijo
de un prado lateral borroso, de una triste
sauceda, una vertiente perdida, un separado
río de solitarios rumores o una playa,
elijo lo que más me revive llamándome.

Pero esta noche, ahora,
esta noche de australes ventanas sacudidas,
tuerzo en el viento malo de primavera, doblo
sus sopladas esquinas y entumecido caigo
en medio de un agónico noviembre.

He aquí la capital mordida, la acechada
de las veinte mil puertas por donde no entró nadie.
Me es dulce al mismo tiempo que me hace arder en llanto
saber que por la tarde puedo siempre abrir una.

Ésta es la dilatada galería, el querido
salón para los ojos de la infancia del sueño.
Oigo mis pasos, miro como nunca mis huellas
retratarse en el polvo de los ecos vacíos.

Es agua a la memoria marchar poniendo nombres
por los desiertos muros que tantos sostuvieron.
Hay sombras coronadas que no están, inasibles

RETURNING TO A DESERTED MUSEUM

Something remains to me when I'm alone, and
taking the path of the heart, climbing
the steep incline of memory, I choose
from a blurred sweep of meadow, from a desolate
willow, a lost hillside, the fork
of a river murmuring to itself, or a beach—
I choose the one that calls me back to life.

But tonight, this time,
on this night with the south windows shaking,
I twist in an ill wind of Spring, I round
its gusting corners, go numb, and fall
into the middle of an agonized November.

War-time Madrid: worn-out, spied on,
with twenty thousand doors that no one enters.
It's sweet, yet makes me flame with grief, to know
that in the evening, I can always open one.

Inside is the vast gallery, the much-loved hall
that used to give our eyes back childhood's dream.
I hear my echoing steps, I see the strange sight
of my footprints in the dust, this emptiness.

It's like watering my memory to walk round putting names
to the deserted walls that used to hold so many.
There are shadows wearing crowns who are not here, solitary

caballos solos, nimbos
de encendidas cabezas cortadas, armaduras
por donde puede el aire salir y entrar al aire,
yelmos desfallecidos, guanteletes sin manos.

Quiero sentarme, busco
descansar como en otros tiempos frente a la ansiada
selva de las audaces diosas desprevenidas,
separar con el mismo temblor del fauno el verde
volante de las hojas que las veda a mi anhelo.

Voy de espacio en espacio,
de vestigio en vestigio,
de silencio en silencio de señales, recorro
los inertes cuadrados ciegos, y le pregunto
a la luz por la vida que los habitó, y lloro
esperanzado, lloro
hasta por las profundas cuencas de los oídos.

Pero no, que una larga soledad un penumbra
es sólo el habitante miedoso de estos ámbitos
donde una muchedumbre de pupilas se enciende,
resbalando, invisible,
por las denunciadoras paredes despobladas.

ghost horses, haloes
of heads cut off and set on fire, armor
permeable even by air, helmets
fallen away, and gauntlets without hands.

I want to sit down, to pause
as in the old days, by the forest pool
where the goddesses bathe, unaware,
to tremble like the faun, and slowly part
the leaves that curtain them from my desire.

I go from room to room,
from vestige to vestige,
from silence to visual silence, I cross through
the inanimate blind squares, and ask the light
about the life that used to dwell here, and I weep,
having hoped a little, I weep until even
the hollows of my ears are cupping tears.

Because loneliness alone resides here,
fearful, in the half-light,
where a multitude of pupils glows
and slides invisibly
across the stripped, accusing walls.

NUEVOS RETORNOS DEL OTOÑO

Nos dicen: Sed alegres.
Que no escuchen los hombres rodar en vuestros cantos
ni el más leve ruido de una lágrima.
Está bien. Yo quisiera, diariamente lo quiero,
mas hay horas, hay días, hasta meses y años
en que se carga el alma de una justa tristeza
y por tantos motivos que luchan silenciosos
rompe a llorar, abiertas las llaves de los ríos.

Miro el otoño, escucho sus aguas melancólicas
de dobladas umbrías que pronto van a irse.
Me miro a mí, me escucho esta mañana
y perdido ese miedo
que me atenaza a veces hasta dejarme mudo,
me repito: Confiesa,
grita valientemente que quisieras morirte.

Di también: Tienes frío.
Di también: Estás solo, aunque otros te acompañen.
¿Qué sería de ti si al cabo no volvieras?
Tus amigos, tu niña, tu mujer, todos esos
que parecen quererte de verdad, ¿qué dirían?

Sonreíd. Sed alegres. Cantad la vida nueva.
Pero yo sin vivirla, ¡cuántas veces la canto!
¡Cuántas veces animo ciegamente a los tristes,
diciéndoles: Sed fuertes, porque vuestra es el alba!

Perdonadme que hoy sienta pena y la diga.
No me culpéis. Ha sido
la vuelta del otoño.

RETURNING TO AUTUMN AGAIN

They say to us: Be happy. Don't listen
to reminding voices rolling through your songs,
or to the small sound of a falling tear.
It's okay. I wish I could, I wish it every day,
but there are hours, days, whole months and even years
when my heart is so heavy with justified sadness
—how many reasons it has—that it breaks,
and the key is turned that opens up the rivers.

I stare out at Autumn, I hear its melancholy waters
throughout groves doubled by leaves soon to be gone.
I stare at myself, I hear myself this morning;
I've lost that fear that sometimes
grips so tight it makes me mute,
so I tell myself: Confess,
be brave, say it out loud, you wish to die.

Say too: You are cold.
Say: You are alone, even with others at your side.
What would happen to you if you never went back?
Your friends, your child, your wife, all those
who seem to love you—what would they all say?

Smile. Be happy. Sing of a new life.
But how often have I sung it without living it!
How often I've scraped bottom giving heart
to the despairing, saying: Be strong, because the dawn is yours!

Forgive me if today I feel only grief, and say so.
Don't blame me. It's because
Autumn's come back.

Part Two

RETURNOS DE AMOR

LOVE RETURNS

RETORNOS DEL AMOR RECIÉN APARECIDO

Cuando tú apareciste,
penaba yo en la entraña más profunda
de una cueva sin aire y sin salida.
Braceaba en lo oscuro, agonizando,
oyendo un estertor que aleteaba
como el latir de un ave imperceptible.
Sobre mí derramaste tus cabellos
y ascendí al sol y vi que eran la aurora
cubriendo un alto mar en primavera.
Fue como si llegara al más hermoso
puerto del mediodía. Se anegaban
en ti los más lúcidos paisajes:
claros, agudos montes coronados
de nieve rosa, fuentes escondidas
en el rizado umbroso de los bosques.

Yo aprendí a descansar sobre sus hombros
y a descender por ríos y laderas,
a entrelazarme en las tendidas ramas
y a hacer del sueño mi más dulce muerte.
Arcos me abriste y mis floridos años
recién subidos a la luz, yacieron
bajo el amor de tu apretada sombra,
sacando el corazón al viento libre
y ajustándolo al verde son del tuyo.
Ya iba a dormir, ya a despertar sabiendo
que no penaba en una cueva oscura,
braceando sin aire y sin salida.

Porque habías al fin aparecido.

LOVE RETURNS AS IT FIRST APPEARED

When you appeared,
I was suffering in the depths
of a cave with no air, no way out.
I flailed in the dark, struggling,
hearing a death-rattle, a last fluttering
like the wingbeats of some unseen bird.
Then your hair spilled down over me
and I rose to the sun and saw your blond dawn
spreading over the high seas of springtime.
It was as if I'd arrived at the loveliest
port of the South. Into you
flowed all the brightest landscapes:
clear, sharp peaks crowned
with roseate snow, and fountains hidden
in the tendrilled shade of the forest.

I learned to lean against your shoulder,
to go down over rivers and slopes,
to entwine myself with boughs spread wide
and to turn sleep into a sweet death.
You opened archways for me, and my young years,
now turned to flowers, lay down
beneath the pressing shadow of your love,
releasing my heart into the open air
and tuning it to the green music of your own.
Now I could fall asleep, now wake up knowing
that I wasn't suffering in a dark cave,
struggling, with no air and no way out.

Because at last, you had appeared.

RETORNOS DEL AMOR EN UN PALCO DE TEATRO

Fuera, en la sala, músicas y luces,
fingido amor, amor que se da en yelo,
en letra muerta, aunque aparentemente
cante sangrando el corazón la vida.

Apagado, llegaba entre cortinas,
oros falsos y rojos terciopelos, el grito
del héroe agonizante a la secreta sombra
del antepalco en donde
el amor verdadero, sin palabras,
sin preparados gestos, sucedía.

Eran dulces las manos y los ojos
adivinados, la tibieza umbrosa
de la piel, las rizadas
oscuridades y el silencio lánguido
en la amorosa escena
que los dos, sin aplausos, ofrecíamos
tan sólo al goce de un espejo mudo.

¡Ah, gracia de los años, maravilla
de ofrecerle al amor cualquier penumbra,
la de un coche, una esquina solitaria
o la de un palco de teatro mientras
puede, sin verla, hasta pasar la muerte!

LOVE RETURNS IN A THEATER-BOX

Outside, in the concert hall, music and lights,
pretended love which came off stiff and frozen,
a dead letter, though supposedly the song
poured from a heart bleeding, aflame.

Faintly, entering between red velvet
curtains edged with imitation gold, the cry
of the dying hero reached the secret
shadow of the box where
without any grand gestures, without words,
real love was taking place.

Our play of hands was sweet, and your
divining eyes, the enshadowed warmth
of your skin, the plush, enfolding
darkness, the mute languor
of the love scene which
we two, without applause, performed
for the sole pleasure of the silent mirror.

Ah the magic of those years, that time of grace
when any darkened place might conjure love—
a secluded corner, a backseat, or a theater-box
where outside, death itself might come,
then go, and we would never know!

RETORNOS DEL AMOR EN LOS BALCONES

Ha llegado ese tiempo en que los años,
las horas, los minutos, los segundos vividos
se perfilan de ti, se llenan de nosotros,
y se hace urgente, se hace necesario,
para no verlos irse con la muerte,
fijar en ellos nuestras más dichosas,
sucesivas imágenes.

¿Dónde estás hoy, en dónde te contemplo,
en qué roca, en qué mar, bajo qué bosque,
o en qué penumbra de estivales sábanas
o en qué calientes, nórdicas alcobas?

Ha pasado la siesta dulce de los azules
que la ancha isla nos tendió en el sueño.
Venus casi dormida aún, te asomas
al íntimo refugio de los barcos
y toda tú ya cantas como un puerto
amoroso de velas y de mástiles.

Tus cabellos tendidos vuelan de los balcones
a enredarse en la trama delgada de las redes,
a poner banderines en los palos más altos
y un concierto de amor en los marinos aires.

Luego, cuando al poniente retornan silenciosos,
blancos de sales y alas de gaviotas,
pongo en tu corazón desnudo mis oídos
y escucho el mar y aspiro el mar que fluye
de ti y me embarco hacia la abierta noche.

LOVE RETURNS ON THE BALCONY

The time has arrived when the years,
the hours, the minutes, the lived-out seconds
all bear the lineaments of your face, are all
suffused with us, and to keep them
from blurring together or fading away,
we need to fix fast in them
images of our times of greatest joy.

Where are you today, where shall I think of you,
on what rock, in what sea or forest,
what cool half-light of summer sheets,
or cozy Northern bedroom?

The sweet siesta hour has just passed, tinged
with the blues the island gave us for our dreams.
Like Venus half-asleep, you're looking out the window
at the intimate, small shelter for the boats,
and coming awake, you start to sing
about a port in love with masts and sails.

On the balcony, your hair flies out, away,
gets tangled in the thin weave of the nets,
sets little flags up in the highest masts,
gets scored into the love song of the breeze.

When you come back in at sunset, your hair
white with the touch of salt and seagulls' wings,
I lay my ear against your naked heart and listen
to the sea, and I inhale the sea that flows
from you, and I embark then for the open night.

RETORNOS DEL AMOR TAL COMO ERA

Eras en aquel tiempo rubia y grande,
sólida espuma ardiente y levantada.
Parecías un cuerpo desprendido
de los centros del sol, abandonado
por un golpe de mar en las arenas.

Todo era fuego en aquel tiempo. Ardía
la playa en tu contorno. A rutilantes
vidrios de luz quedaban reducidos
las algas, los moluscos y las piedras
que el oleaje contra ti mandaba.

Todo era fuego, exhalación, latido
de onda caliente en ti. Si era una mano
la atrevida o los labios, ciegas ascuas,
voladoras, silbaban por el aire.
Tiempo abrasado, sueño consumido.

Yo me volqué en tu espuma en aquel tiempo.

LOVE RETURNS AS IT ONCE WAS

In those days you were statuesque and golden,
risen out of sea-foam, glittering.
You seemed a body flung out
from the center of the sun, abandoned
by a billow on the sand.

Everything was fire in those days. Around you,
the beach blazed. Seaweed, mollusks,
pebbles sent against you by the surf—
all were reduced
to flashing shards of light.

Everything was fire, shooting stars, the beat
of the wave of heat inside you. Whether
my hand began it, or your lips,
blind sparks, flying, whistled through the air.
Season of flame, of dreams fully consumed.

Your dazzling foam engulfed me in those days.

RETORNOS DEL AMOR EN UNA AZOTEA

Poblado estoy de muchas azoteas.
Sobre la mar se tienden las más blancas,
dispuestas a zarpar al sol, llevando
como velas las sábanas tendidas.
Otras dan a los campos, pero hay una
que sólo da al amor, cara a los montes.
Y es la que siempre vuelve.

Allí el amor peinaba sus geranios,
conducía las rosas y jazmines
por las barandas y en la ardiente noche
se deshacía en una fresca lluvia.

Lejos, las cumbres, soportando el peso
de las grandes estrellas, lo velaban.
¿Cuándo el amor vivió más venturoso
ni cuándo entre las flores
recién regadas fuera
con más alma en la sangre poseído?

Subía el silbo de los trenes. Tiemblos
de farolillos de verbena y músicas
de los kioscos y encendidos árboles
remontaban y súbitos diluvios
de cometas veloces que vertían
en sus ojos fugaces resplandores.

Fue la más bella edad del corazón. Retorna
hoy tan distante en que la estoy soñando
sobre este viejo tronco, en un camino
que no me lleva ya a ninguna parte.

LOVE RETURNS UP ON THE ROOF

I am a man of many rooftops.
The whitest ones are set above the sea,
ready to cast off for the sun, bearing
like sails their sheets hung out to dry.
Others open onto fields, but one, though it looks out
to mountains, opens only onto love.
It's this roof that returns to me the most.

There love tied back the tendrils of geraniums,
trailed the jasmine and the rose along the rail,
and in the burning night might come undone
in a sudden pouring shower of cooling rain.

Far off, the peaks that bore the weight
of the great stars watched over it.
When was love ever so lucky,
and when, amidst just-sprinkled
petals, possessed
with such force by the blood?

Train whistles floated up. Tremblings
of Chinese lanterns from the fairs, live
music, and the glow of lighted trees; these all
rose up, while comets came cascading down,
filling love's eyes in a flash
of fleeting splendor.

It was the sweetest epoch of my heart.
It all returns to me today, so distant
from where I am now, dreaming on this stump
beside a road that opens onto nothing.

RETORNOS DEL AMOR ANTE LAS ANTIGUAS DEIDADES

Soñarte, amor, soñarte como entonces,
ante aquellas Dianas desceñidas,
aquellas diosas de robustos pechos
y el viento impune entre las libres piernas.

Tú eras lo mismo, amor. Todas las Gracias,
igual que tres veranos encendidos,
el levantado hervor de las bacantes,
la carrera bullente de las ninfas,
esa maciza flor de la belleza
redonda y clara, poderosamente
en ti se abría, en ti también se alzaba.

Soñarte como entonces, sí, soñarte
ante aquellas fundidas alamedas,
jardín de Amor en donde la ancha Venus,
muslos dorados, vientre pensativo,
se baña en el concierto de la tarde.

Soñarte, amor, soñarte, oh, sí, soñarte
la idéntica de entonces, la surgida
del mar y aquellos bosques, reviviendo
en ti el amor henchido, sano y fuerte
de las antiguas diosas terrenales.

LOVE RETURNS AMID THE ANCIENT DEITIES

Love, let me dream of you as you were then,
wandering amid Dianas all undressed,
those full-breasted goddesses, between whose legs
only the wind moved with impunity.

You were their equal. All the Graces,
like three glowing summers,
the boiling fervor of the maenads,
the laughing race run by the nymphs,
that multi-petaled flower of beauty,
cupped and bright, opened
in you, too, rose up in you.

Yes, let me dream of you as you were then,
amid the blended silver of the poplars,
in the Garden of Love, where Venus, voluptuous
with golden thighs and meditative belly, bathed
in a concert of afternoon light.

O let me dream of you, love, dream of you
the same as then, arisen from the sea
and woods, the full, intense love
of the ancient earthly goddesses
alive again in you.

RETORNOS DEL AMOR EN LAS DUNAS RADIANTES

¡Oh, vuelve, sí, retorna la de aquellas mañanas
radiantes de los médanos,
la desnuda y caliente de las solas arenas,
como un ancho oleaje de espuma revolcada,
de enfurecido sol siempre agitado!

¡Oh, sí, vuelve, retorna como entonces, tendida,
con tus rubios cabellos de ángel entre los pechos,
con tus dulces declives resbalando
hacia las más rizadas penumbras sumergidas!

¡Oh, ser joven, ser joven, ser joven! No te vayas,
vuelve, vuelve, retorna, retorna a mí esta tarde,
en estas solitarias dunas donde las olas
rompen con los perfiles de tus hondos costados,
donde el batido mar tiende piernas azules,
mece labios que cantan
y brazos ya nocturnos que me ciñen y llevan.

LOVE RETURNS IN THE RADIANT DUNES

O return her, bring her back, the one
from those radiant days in the dunes,
naked and hot on the secluded sand,
like a full, breaking wave
flung down by a furious sun!

O yes, come back as you were then,
stretched out, blond hair like an angel's
falling over your breasts, your sweet curves sliding
towards rippling undersea shadows!

O to be young, to be young, to be young! Don't go,
come back, return to me this afternoon,
in these solitary dunes where the receding tide
imprints your outline on the beach,
where the beating sea spreads its blue legs,
rocking me with lips that sing, and arms
that hold me and enfold me like the night.

RETORNOS DEL AMOR EN LOS BOSQUES NOCTURNOS

¡Son los bosques, los bosques que regresan! Aquellos
donde el amor, volcado, se pinchaba en las zarzas
y era como un arroyo feliz, encandecido
de pequeñas estrellas de dulcísima sangre.

Los bosques de la noche, con el amor callado,
sintiendo solamente el latir de las hojas,
el profundo compás de los pechos hundidos
y el temblor de la tierra y el cielo en las espaldas.

¡Qué consuelo sin nombre no perder la memoria,
tener llenos los ojos de los tiempos pasados,
de las noches aquellas en que el amor ardía
como el único dios que habitaba los bosques!

LOVE RETURNS AT NIGHT IN THE WOODS

It's the woods, those woods, that come back to me,
where love, turned over, pricked itself on the brambles,
happily becoming a small stream, shiny
with tiny star-marks of sweet blood.

Those woods at night, with love fallen silent,
feeling only the thrumming of the leaves,
the deep rhythm of us sunk into each other,
and the trembling at our backs of earth and sky.

What a solace to have kept my memory,
to be able to fill my eyes with vanished time,
with those nights when love glittered and burned
like the only god inhabiting the woods!

RETORNOS DEL AMOR EN UNA NOCHE DE VERANO

A tientas el amor, a ciegas en lo oscuro,
tal vez entre las ramas, madura, alguna estrella,
vuelvo a sentirlo, vuelvo,
mojado de la escarcha caliente de la noche,
contra el hoyo de mentas tronchadas y tomillos.

Es él, único, solo, lo mismo que mi mano,
la piel desparramada de mi cuerpo, la sombra
de mi recién salido corazón, los umbrosos
centros más subterráneos de mi ser lo querían.

Vuelve único, vuelve
como forma tocada nada más, como llena
palpitación tendida cubierta de cabellos,
como sangre enredada en mi sangre, un latido
dentro de otro latido solamente.

Mas las palabras, ¿dónde?
Las palabras no llegan. No tuvieron espacio
en aquel agostado nocturno, no tuvieron
ese mínimo aire que media entre dos bocas
antes de reducirse a un clavel silencioso.

Pero un aroma oculto se desliza, resbala,
me quema un desvelado olor a oscura orilla.
Alguien está prendiendo por la yerba un murmullo.
Es que siempre en la noche del amor pasa un río.

LOVE RETURNS ON A SUMMER NIGHT

Tentatively, love comes, blindly in the dark,
maybe a star ripening in the branches,
I go back so I can feel it, back,
wet with the warm dew of the night, pressed
into a hollow of crushed mint and thyme.

It's not like anything, it's what my hand,
the skin over the whole length of my frame, the shadow
of my newly risen heart, the subterranean
center of my being most desired.

It's come back, transformative, and then
there's just the shape that I am touching, we're
enveloped by her hair, all one pulsation,
blood entangled too, a heartbeat felt
inside another heartbeat.

But words—where have they gone?
No words. No air for them to occupy
in this parched August night, not even
that little space that separates two mouths
before it shrinks into a silent flower.

But a secret fragrance wafts up, gliding by, a scent
awakened on the dark bank scorches me.
Someone lights a murmur in the grass. Always
on a night of love, a river's flowing past.

RETORNOS DEL AMOR EN LOS VIVIDOS PAISAJES

Creemos, amor mío, que aquellos paisajes
se quedaron dormidos o muertos con nosotros
en la edad, en el día en que los habitamos;
que los árboles pierden la memoria
y las noches se van, dando al olvido
lo que las hizo hermosas y tal vez inmortales.

Pero basta el más leve palpitar de una hoja,
una estrella borrada que respira de pronto
para vernos los mismos alegres que llenamos
 los lugares que juntos nos tuvieron.
Y así despiertas hoy, mi amor, a mi costado,
entre los groselleros y las fresas ocultas
al amparo del firme corazón de los bosques.

Allí está la caricia mojada de rocío,
las briznas delicadas que refrescan tu lecho,
los silfos encantados de ornar tu cabellera
y las altas ardillas misteriosas que llueven
sobre tu sueño el verde menudo de las ramas.

Sé feliz, hoja, siempre: nunca tengas otoño,
hoja que me has traído
con tu temblor pequeño
el aroma de tanta ciega edad luminosa.

LOVE RETURNS TO LANDSCAPES STILL ALIVE

We believe, love, that those landscapes are asleep
or dead, along with us, their true life locked
away back in the days we spent in them;
we believe the trees have lost their memory,
the nights have thinned and given away
whatever made them beautiful and timeless.

But it takes just the slightest trembling of a leaf,
the sudden breathing of a burnt-out star,
to find ourselves the same ones whose delight
filled the places that held fast our own embrace.
And so today, love, you awaken at my side,
among wild currants and hidden strawberries,
protected by the staunch heart of the forest.

Here is the wet kiss of the dew,
the tender blades of grass that cool your bed,
the enchanted sylphs who decorate your hair,
and the high, mysterious squirrels whose play rains down
the green small-change of branches on your sleep.

Leaf, may you always be happy and
never know autumn, leaf whose slight
trembling carried back to me
the fragrance of those blind and luminous days.

Y tú, mínima estrella perdida que me abres
las íntimas ventanas de mis noches más jóvenes,
nunca cierres tu lumbre
sobre tantas alcobas que al alba nos durmieron
y aquella biblioteca con la luna
y los libros aquellos dulcemente caídos
y los montes afuera desvelados cantándonos.

And you, lost star, who opened up for me
an intimate window onto my youngest nights,
may you never stop shining
on all the beds we slept in until dawn,
and that library lit by the moon,
and those books fallen quietly open,
and the mountains outside, awake and singing to us.

RETORNOS DEL AMOR FUGITIVO EN LOS MONTES

Era como una isla de Teócrito. Era
la edad de oro de las olas. Iba
a alzarse Venus de la espuma. Era
la edad de oro de los campos. Iba
Pan nuevamente a repetir su flauta
y Príapo a verterse en los jardines.
Todo era entonces. Todo entonces iba.

Iba el amor a ser dichoso. Era
la juventud con cinco toros dentro.
Iba el ardor a arder en los racimos.
Era la sangre un borbotón de llamas.
Era la paz para el amor. Venía
la edad de oro del amor. Ya era.

Pero en la isla aparecieron barcos
y hombres armados en las playas. Venus
no fue alumbrada por la espuma. El aire
en la flauta de Pan se escondió, mudo.
Secas, las flores sin su dios murieron
y el amor, perseguido, huyó a los montes.

Allí labró su cueva, como errante
hijo arrojado de una mar oscura,
entre el mortal y repetido estruendo
que la asustada Eco devolvía.

Agujas rotas de los parasoles

LOVE RETURNS AS A FUGITIVE IN THE MOUNTAINS

It was an island straight out of Theocritus. It was
the golden age of waves. Venus
was about to rise out of the foam. It was
the golden age of fields. Pan
was about to play his pipe again
and Priapus spill himself deep in the garden.
Everything had come together. It was all about to happen.

Love was soon to be delighted. Young,
with five bulls inside.
Passion blazed in the grape-clusters.
Veins flowed with flame. Peace
existed for love. The golden age
of love approached. Had come.

But then ships appeared off the island
and armed men on the beach. Venus
was not born from the foam. The tune
in Pan's flute hid itself, gone mute.
Without their god, the flowers shrivelled and died,
and love, pursued, fled up into the mountains.

There, like a wandering exile cast up
by the sea, it made its den
amid a constant deadly uproar
that frightened even Echo to repeat.

Fallen needles from the parasol pines

pinos le urdieron al amor su lecho.
Fieras retamas, mustias madreselvas,
rudos hinojos y áridos tomillos
lo enguirnaldaron en la ciega noche.
Y aunque, lengua de fuego, el aire aullara
alrededor, la tierra, oh, sí, la tierra
no le fue dura, sin embargo, al sueño
del fugitivo amor entre los montes.

La edad de oro del amor venía,
pero en la isla aparecieron barcos...

fashioned a bed for love.
Wild broom and faded honeysuckle,
rough fennel and dried thyme
adorned the bed with garlands in the night.
And even if, all around, the air
howled in the language of fire, the earth
was not too hard for love,
a fugitive now, in the mountains.

The golden age of love had come,
but off the island, ships appeared...

RETORNOS DEL AMOR EN LA NOCHE TRISTE

Ven, amor mío, ven, en esta noche
sola y triste de Italia. Son tus hombros
fuertes y bellos los que necesito.
Son tus preciosos brazos, la largura
maciza de tus muslos y ese arranque
de pierna, esa compacta
línea que te rodea y te suspende,
dichoso mar, abierta playa mía.
¿Cómo decirte, amor, en esta noche
solitaria de Génova, escuchando
el corazón azul del oleaje,
que eres tú la que vienes por la espuma?
Bésame, amor, en esta noche triste.
Te diré las palabras que mis labios,
de tanto amor, mi amor, no se atrevieron.
Amor mío, amor mío, es tu cabeza
de oro tendido junto a mí, su ardiente
bosque largo de otoño quien me escucha.
Óyeme, que te llamo. Vida mía,
sí, vida mía, vida mía sola.
¿De quién más, de quién más si solamente
puedo ser yo quien cante a tus oídos:
vida, vida, mi vida, vida mía?
¿Qué soy sin ti, mi amor? Dime qué fuera
sin ese fuerte y dulce muro blando
que me da luz cuando me da la sombra,
sueño, cuando se escapa de mis ojos.
Yo no puedo dormir. ¡Cuántas auroras,

LOVE RETURNS IN THE SAD NIGHT

Come to me, love, come on this sad
Italian night. It's your beautiful
strong shoulders that I need,
your lovely arms, your long
and solid thighs, your springing
legs, that magic line,
encircling you and holding you,
blissful sea, my open shore.
O love, how do I let you know
on this lonely night in Genoa, listening
to the blue heart of the surf,
that you're the one who rises from the foam?
Kiss me, love, on this sad night.
I'll tell you all the words my lips,
so full of love, did not dare say.
My love, my love, when your golden head
lies next to mine, I feel its flaming,
long, autumnal forest listening.
So hear me now, I'm calling you. My life,
yes, my life, my only life.
Who else? Who else, if I'm
the only one whose song can reach your ears:
life, my very life, my life?
What am I without you, love? What would I be
without that sweet, strong wall, so soft,
that gives me light when it enshadows me,
dream, when it escapes my eyes.
Here, I can't sleep. How many more

oscuras, braceando en las tinieblas,
sin encontrarte, amor! ¡Cuántos amargos
golpes de sal, sin ti, contra mi boca!
¿Dónde estás? ¿Dónde estás? Dime, amor mío.
¿Me escuchas? ¿No me sientes
llegar como una lágrima llamándote,
por encima del mar, en esta noche?

dark dawns, love, when I flail around
in blackness and can't find you? How many
bitter blows of salt against my mouth?
Where are you? Where are you? Tell me now.
Do you hear me? Don't you feel me
approaching you like tears, calling you
over the sea, in the night?

RETORNOS DEL AMOR EN MEDIO DEL MAR

Esplendor mío, amor,
inicial de mi vida,
quiero decirte toda tu belleza,
aquí, en medio del mar, cuando voy en tu busca,
cuando tan sólo puedo compararte
con la hermosura tibia de las olas.
Es tu cabeza un manantial de oro,
una lluvia de espuma dorada que me enciende
y lleva a navegar al fondo de la noche.
Es tu frente la aurora con dos arcos
por los que pasan dulces esos soles
con que sueñan al alba los navíos.
¿Qué decir de tu boca y tus orejas,
de tu cuello y tus hombros si el mar esconde conchas,
corales y jardines sumergidos
que quisieran al soplo
de las alas del sur ser como ellos?
Son tus costados como dos lejanas
bahías en reposo
donde al son de tus brazos sólo canta
el silencio de amor que las rodea.
Triste es hablar, cuando se está distante,
de los golfos de sombra, de las islas
que llaman al marino que los siente
pasar, sin verlos, fuera de su ruta.
Amor mío, tus piernas son dos playas,
dos médanos tendidos que se elevan
con un rumor de juncos si no duermen.

LOVE RETURNS IN THE MIDDLE OF THE SEA

My radiance, my love,
origin of my life,
I want to tell you all your beauty,
here, in the middle of the sea, where I seek you,
where I can only compare you
to the cool splendor of the waves.
Your hair is a fountain of gold,
a shining shower that inflames me, and leads me
to sail to the depths of the night.
Your brow is a dawn with two rainbows
through whose arches sail sweet suns
of which the boats all dream until first light.
What more can I say of your mouth, your ears,
your neck and shoulders, than that the sea
hides its shells, its corals and submarine gardens
lest, inspired by the wings of the South,
they fashion themselves after you?
Your sides form two still bays
where the music of your arms
is the only song sung
by the silence of love that enfolds them.
It is sad to speak from a distance
of those gulfs of shadow, those islands
that call to the passing sailor, who can
sense them, though they lie outside his view.
My love, your legs are two beaches,
two long dunes alive with
a murmur of rushes, unless they're asleep.

Dame tus pies pequeños para andarte,
para sentirte todas tus riberas.
Voy por el mar, voy sobre ti, mi vida,
sobre tu amor, hacia tu amor, cantando
tu belleza más bella que las olas.

Give me your little feet so I can wander
over you, and explore every shore.
I travel over the sea, I travel over you, my life,
through your love, towards your love, singing
your beauty, more splendid than the waves.

RETORNOS DEL AMOR EN LOS ANTIGUOS CALLEJONES

Queda siempre la dicha, el infinito
don de poder tornar sobre los pasos
distantes que pusimos en aquellos lugares
que nuestro amor lo mismo que en un sueño
nos fue creando.
                                    Ahora
es el delgado, oscuro laberinto
de una ciudad dormida, un agrietado
corazón donde un río lame y canta
la silenciosa noche de las piedras.

Había que estrecharse hasta los dos ser uno
para poder entrar en tanto enredo
de esquinas, puertas, patios y balcones.
Nunca el amor llegó más a lo hondo
de los pasados siglos.
                                    Caballeros,
como llamas exangües, como extintos
fuegos fatuos surgían, apagándose.

Me vi de pronto que estrechaba a Débora,
a Judit o a Raquel, la más hermosa,
suelto el cabello, en el brocal del pozo.
¡Amor, amor, amor! Amor tornándose,
nuevo clavel, en fresca flor antigua,
rosa de aljama, aroma de los huertos
de Jericó, o Zulema,
la cautiva en la torre
del arrabal indómito del río.

LOVE RETURNS IN ANCIENT ALLEYWAYS

Always there remains the joy, the infinite
gift of being able to go back
over the distant steps we took in all
those places love created round us
like a dream.
                    Now:
the darkened, narrow maze
of a sleeping city, a heart
cracked open where a river sings and laps against
a silent night of stones.

We two drew close, almost becoming one,
in order to pass through into that tangle
of patios, corners, balconies, and doors.
Never had love found itself so deep
inside the past.
                    Noblemen
like bloodless flames, tenuous
will-o'-the-wisps, flared and died away.

Suddenly, it seemed I was walking with Deborah,
or Judith, or Rachel, the most beautiful of all,
long hair falling, glancing down into the well.
Love, love! Love transforming itself,
bright carnation, into an ancient fresh flower,
rose of the synagogue, perfume
of the gardens of Jericho, Zulema,
the captive in the tower
in that wilderness beyond the river.

¿Cómo volver, amor, a la que fuiste?
¿Por dónde la salida, si hasta el aire,
prisionero, gemía por hallarla?

Llantos sinagogales, moribundos
ayes de las desérticas arenas
e insomnes, gregorianos
lamentos en las débiles
luces de las penumbras enclaustradas,
más nos perdían, sin posible oriente,
hasta que al fin los cantos chirriados
de los madrugadores arrieros
desenredaron nuestro andar, llevándonos
a las fluviales arboledas, donde
ya libres, con el alba,
ennochecimos en un claro sueño.

Love, how do we get back to what we were?
How do we get back, when even the air,
imprisoned here, howls for an exit?

Weeping kaddishes, dying
moans from the deserted arenas,
and insomniac, Gregorian
laments in the feeble
light leaking from penumbral cloisters
all got us further lost, disoriented,
'til finally the chirruping songs
of early-rising muleteers
unravelled our way, and led us
to the fluvial groves where
free now, with the dawn,
we fell into a spacious sleep.

RETORNOS DEL ÁNGEL DE SOMBRA

A veces, amor mío, soy tu ángel de sombra.
Me levanto de no sé qué guaridas,
fulmíneo, entre los dientes
una espada de filos amargos, una triste
espada que tú bien, mi pobre amor, conoces.
Son los días oscuros de la furia, las horas
del despiadado despertar, queriéndote
en medio de las lágrimas subidas
del más injusto y dulce desconsuelo.
Yo sé, mi amor, de dónde esas tinieblas
vienen a mí, ciñéndote, aprentándome
hasta hacerlas caer sobre tus hombros
y doblarlos, deshechos como un río.
¿Qué quieres tú, si a veces, amor mío, así soy,
cuando en las imborrables piedras pasadas, ciego,
me destrozo y batallo por romperlas,
por verte libre y sola en la luz mía?
Vencido siempre, aniquilado siempre,
vuelvo a la calma, amor, a la serena
felicidad, hasta ese oscuro instante
en que de nuevo bajo a mis guaridas
para erguirme otra vez tu ángel de sombra.

THE ANGEL OF DARKNESS RETURNS

Sometimes, beloved, I am your angel of darkness.
I rise from who-knows-what lair, ready
to explode, in place of my tongue
a sword with bitter edges, a
melancholy sword you know too well.
Then come days of dark rage, mornings
of pitiless awakenings, wanting you
in the midst of my despair at the injustice,
that old grief almost sweet.
I know where this darkness comes from, love,
pressing down on me, and crushing
you under its weight, rushing over you
like a violent river.
And so I hurl myself blindly
at the ineradicable rock of the past,
struggling to smash it so you can be
free and returned to the light.
Always defeated, always overcome, in time
I feel calm again, suffused
with serene joy, until that darkened moment
when I wake back in my lair
and your angel of darkness reappears.

RETORNOS DEL AMOR EN LAS ARENAS

Esta mañana, amor, tenemos veinte años.
Van voluntariamente lentas, entrelazándose
nuestras sombras descalzas camino de los huertos
que enfrentan los azules del mar con sus verdores.
Tú todavía eres casi la aparecida,
la llegada una tarde sin luz entre dos luces,
cuando el joven sin rumbo de la ciudad prolonga,
pensativo, a sabiendas el regreso a su casa.
Tú todavía eres aquella que a mi lado
vas buscando el declive secreto de las dunas,
la ladera recóndita de la arena, el oculto
cañaveral que pone
cortinas a los ojos marineros del viento.
Allí estás, allí estoy contra ti, comprobando
la alta temperatura de las olas felices,
el corazón del mar ciegamente ascendido,
muriéndose en pedazos de dulce sal y espumas.
Todo nos mira alegre, después, por las orillas.
Los castillos caídos sus almenas levantan,
las algas nos ofrecen coronas y las velas,
tendido el vuelo, quieren cantar sobre las torres.

Esta mañana, amor, tenemos veinte años.

LOVE RETURNS ON THE SANDS

This morning, my love, we are twenty years old.
Our shadows slowly weave themselves together,
barefoot on the road beside the orchard
facing the sea's blues with all its greens.
You're almost still the one who came that dusk
in the lightless time between the sky's two lights
when a young man, ambling thoughtfully,
deliberately prolonged his walk back home.
You're still the one beside me, seeking
the secret dip of the dunes,
the hidden hollow in the sand, the concealed
cane-beds creating curtains
that block the sailor-gazes of the wind.
There you are, and I am joined to you, taking
the high temperature of the happy waves,
the heart of the sea blindly rising,
dying away in bits of salt and foam.
Afterwards, everything looks at us with joy.
The fallen castles lift their parapets,
the seaweed gives us garlands, and the sails,
spread wide, want to sing out over the towers.

This morning, my love, we are twenty years old.

RETORNOS DEL AMOR ENTRE LAS RUINAS ILUSTRES

Vuelven las piedras calcinadas, vuelven
en derribados templos, en caídos
lupanares, en patios verdes donde
la sonrisa de Príapo calienta
todavía el recuerdo de las fuentes.

Vamos, amor, por calles que se fueron,
por claras geometrías que llevaban
al misterioso amor, a los placeres
vedados, pero dulces en la noche.

Ésta es la casa de la diosa. Aspira
por los azules ámbitos su aroma
a espuma marinera, a los jazmines
y claveles salados de su cuerpo.

El símbolo viril jovial reposa,
en todo su verdor puro, tendido
sobre el plato feliz de la balanza
que le ofrece el Amor. Su peso excede
al de todos los frutos de la tierra.
(Afrodita en penumbra se sonríe,
sintiendo el mar batirle entre los muslos.)

¡Oh claridad antigua, oh luz lejana,
desnuda luz, cúbrenos siempre!
Mas cuando ya ruinas, piedras solas
lleguemos, amor mío, a ser un día,
seamos como estas que al sol cantan
y que al amor conducen por calles que se fueron.

LOVE RETURNS AMIDST THE STORIED RUINS

The calcined stones come back to me,
the toppled temples, fallen brothels,
green courtyards where
the smile of Priapus
still warms a memory of fountains.

Let us go, love, down streets that have fallen away,
whose clear geometry once led
to mysterious love, to pleasures
forbidden, but sweet in the night.

This is the goddess' house. In this
blue space, breathe in
her fragrance: sea-foam, jasmine,
carnations slightly salty from her skin.

The jovial phallus-god reposes
in all his Spring vigor,
stretched out upon the delighted
pan of the scale offered by Love.
Heavier than all the fruits of the earth.
(Aphrodite smiles in the penumbra,
feeling the sea beat between her thighs.)

O ancient radiance, far-distant light, naked
light, love, envelop us always!
But when one day we, too, have become
ruins, my love, only stones,
let us be like these that sing to the sun
and lead to love down streets that have fallen away.

RETORNOS DEL AMOR CON LA LUNA

Tú eras la luna con la luna. Remontabas
del fatigado lecho, tan grande y reluciente,
que las dormidas sábanas oscuras se creían
ser las alumbradoras de un sol desconocido.

Profunda, era la alcoba como un aljibe inmóvil
que subiera encantado de un agua iluminada.
Nadaban sumergidas en dulce luz las ondas
que tus brazos hacían morir contra los muros.

Cuando al fin ascendías a los altos cristales
que la luna remota ya con sueño miraba,
tú, luna con la luna, rebosando, caías
nuevamente apagada en tu lecho tranquilo.

Otras cosas la luna me trajo en esta noche,
al subir, solitaria, sobre los mudos árboles.

LOVE RETURNS WITH THE MOON

You were another moon beneath the moon. You rose
from our weary bed, so huge and shining
that the darkened sleepy sheets thought they'd become
the source of light for a mysterious sun.

The quiet cistern of our room became a fountain,
enchanted by the dazzle on its water.
Waves formed in the soft light; when you raised
your arms, they broke against the walls.

When at last you climbed to the upper windowpanes
which the moon, now distant, gazed at sleepily,
you, my moon accompanying the moon, overflowing,
fell back again, extinguished, into bed.

The moon has brought me other things tonight,
rising, alone, over the silent trees.

RETORNOS DEL AMOR EN LAS CUMBRES DEL VIENTO

Vienes ahora, amor, precedida del viento
que las rubias llanuras de pan recién florido
en las templadas horas
de aquel nuestro inicial estío levantaron
para hacerte más alta y encendida en las piedras.

Cimbrabas en el fino cauce del monumento
de similares arcos que las manos romanas
tendieron por encima de los templos y torres
de la ciudad, pensando tal vez en que algún día
lo coronaras tú con los pequeños pasos
de tu ardiente blancura.

Recibías, en medio de aquel pétreo zumbido
de osamenta sonora clavada en los espacios,
la cara de la luz que en los pelados montes
se empinaba, los pueblos de pálidos ladrillos,
los senderos quemados, la dormida grandeza,
en fin, de un paisaje atónito de verte
como la aparecida de las cumbres del viento.

¡Ah, poder, amor mío, de pronto, contemplarte
de nuevo, como entonces,
a aquella misma altura de sol, dando a las horas
de nuestro inaugural verano la armonía,
toda esa clara música encendida que fuiste
sobre aquel fino cauce de las antiguas piedras!
¡Y poder nuevamente, ya entrados en la noche,
descender y en la dulce oscuridad tendidos
alzar de tiempo en tiempo la cabeza, mirando
por los vacíos arcos tranquilas las estrellas!

LOVE RETURNS ON THE SUMMITS OF THE WIND

You come back, love, preceded by the wind
which rose up from the blond fields of bread
brought to flower during the warm hours
of our first summer, blowing you stalk-
straight and burnished mid the stones.

You swayed on the narrow way beneath
the arches of a monument once set
by Roman hands above the temples and the towers
of their town, with hope, perhaps,
that someday you might crown it
with the gleam of your white steps.

You took to yourself, in the midst of that humming
framework of sonorous stones fixed
in place, the face of light that rose
on the bare mountain, the villages of faded
brick, the burning paths, the sleeping vastness
of a landscape astonished to see you
like an apparition on the summits of the wind.

Ah love, to be able suddenly
to see you once again just like before,
under that same high sun which gave
to our first summer's days their harmony!
All that bright and luminous music that you were,
beneath the arches of those ancient stones!
And to be able, once again, when night arrived,
to go down and lie out in the soft dark,
lifting our heads only occasionally
to gaze through the open arches at the stars!

RETORNOS DEL AMOR ADONDE NUNCA ESTUVO

Si tú, mi amor, subieras a esta torre,
se te entraría con la luz y el viento
toda la verde música que mueven
los campos ascendidos a jardines.

Tus pies serían de maíz y avenas,
de entrelazadas fuentes y rosales;
tus piernas, de bambúes; de amarillos
albérchigos tus muslos, y tus ingles,
de ciruelas lloradas
por ceñir tu cintura.

De álamos blancos y eucaliptos grises,
ligados a los hombros, tus dos pechos,
como dos altos soles, asomando
al mirador movido de las ramas.

¿De qué, mi amor, sería tu cabeza
sino de cielo orlado por los bosques
de todas las estrellas, descendidos
al rubio resonar de tus cabellos?

Sube, mi amor, retorna adonde nunca
estuviste, que quiero en esta noche,
contigo, oír la música que mueven
los campos ascendidos a jardines.

LOVE RETURNS TO A PLACE IT'S NEVER BEEN

If you, my love, could climb up to this tower,
there would flow into you, along with the light
and the wind, all the green music made
by these fields metamorphosed into gardens.

Your feet would become maize and oats,
small rose-bushes braided with fountains;
your legs, slender bamboo; yellow
peaches, your thighs, and your pelvis,
plums weeping,
encircling your waist.

White poplars and grey eucalyptus
would grow from your shoulders, your breasts,
like two high suns, gazing out
from the budding balcony of branches.

And what, my love, would your head become
but a heaven surrounded by
forests of stars, drawn down
by the blond pealing of your hair?

Climb up, my love, come back
to a place you've never been, because tonight
I want to hear with you the music made
by these fields metamorphosed into gardens.

Part Three

RETORNOS DE UN PONIENTE EN RAVELLO

Tú vuelves siempre, y siempre
más claro y perfilado, más maduro
de pleno azul y antigua trasparencia.
Desde allí te veía como ahora,
lejano mar, te miro,
desde esta tarde de otro continente,
colgado en mi memoria, atravesándola
de poniente a levante,
de mediodía a norte.
Tuve yo que escalar aquella fina hondura,
aquel cielo de estatuas y rumores
para abrazarte todo y retenerte.
Abierto, abajo estabas, suspendido
como por invisibles
alas, como llevado
a hombros del aire, entera
levedad, extendida, uniforme hermosura.

Se asomaban los dioses,
las inmóviles formas tutelares,
verdeados de umbría, a las barandas
del detenido ocaso.
Mirado de los pinos, venturoso
de dormirse alabado de las fuentes,
no se marchaba el sol, no, no quería
ponerse el sol, el sol, el sol tendido,
descansado en el mar, balanceado

RETURN OF A SUNSET AT RAVELLO

Always, you come back, and always
more clear and heightened, ripened
to sheer blue and ancient transparency.
I saw the distant sea from there
as now I see it from
this evening on another continent,
suspended in my memory, stretching
across it from east
to west, from north to south.
I also plumbed the depths above—hyaline
sky foregrounded by statues, soft voices—
so I could fully grasp you and retain you.
In the openness below, you hovered
as if on invisible
wings, as if borne
on the shoulders of the air, weightless,
diffusing beauty everywhere.

The gods, constant guardian
deities of that place, still green
from their grove, were beginning to appear
at the overlook of the lingering sunset.
Seen from the pines, that lucky sun,
lulled to sleep by the praise of the fountains,
didn't seem to be leaving; no, it did not want
to set, the sun, the sun, that sun, floating
refreshed on the sea, imperceptibly

imperceptiblemente en las espumas.
Iba en aquel crepúsculo a cumplirse
la completa derrota de la noche;
a fijarse la luz, un milagroso,
perpetuo resplandor, en fin, el día,
el día ya sin muerte.

Desnudada de sombra, era la tierra
quien iba a prolongarse
en la dicha. Era el hombre
sin cuerpo de desastres,
por vez primera libre,
dueño de ser el hombre, melodiosa
carne sin leyes de agonía, puro,
vivo soplo de gracia.

Y aunque quizás no lejos se sintiera
subir como un lenguaje de sílabas de carros,
una invasora rueda de frío estruendo, iban
sobre el azul del mar a inaugurarse
la edad de la tranquila proporción, el ansiado
tiempo del canto luminoso, el sueño
de la diafanidad y la armonía,
de la paz ya sin fin, detenido el poniente.

poised in the foam.
That evening, it was going to accomplish
the utter defeat of the night, and fix
fast the light, creating
a miraculous, unending splendor:
day without death.

It was the earth's wish: uncovered
by shadows, it could prolong
its delight. Human beings
could shake disaster from their bodies, feel
for the first time free, true
owners of themselves, melodious
flesh without statutes of suffering,
each breath an inhalation of pure grace.

And even though one might sense in the distance,
rising like a language whose syllables were tanks,
an invading wheel of cold calamity, still,
above the blue of the sea was about to begin
an age of tranquil symmetry, the longed for
time of luminous song, the dream
of diaphancity and harmony, of peace
now finally without end, the sunset
                              having been stopped.

RETORNOS DE YEHUDA HALEVI, EL CASTELLANO

Te he conocido tarde, poeta, cuando ahora,
en medio del camino de la vida,
oigo de entre mis manos resbalarse,
latido por latido, triste, el tiempo.

Me llega tu perfume,
distante de las tierras y jardines
que tu viajero corazón anduvo.
Te hubiera yo encontrado
en una torcedura callada de Toledo,
melancólicamente, hacia el río. Te hubiera
ofrecido un limón de un patio de Sevilla,
una rama de olivas de Lucena, cantando
contigo entre tinajas al sol, o quizás viendo
irse de sangre derretida en nieve
las cumbres de un ocaso granadino.

Hoy es tu errante aroma,
tu desterrado aliento el que me busca,
romero por el mar, alto, dichoso,
loco de maravilla entre los truenos,
marinero de Dios, arrebatado
sobre un carro de aguas encendidas.

Yo también como tú siento en mi día
el misterioso llamamiento, el aura
invitadora al viaje, y de Occidente,
aparejado el corazón, abierto
de alas cargadas de la noche, al mar,
me hago a la mar, con rumbo a la mañana.

RETURN OF YEHUDA HALEVI, "THE CASTILIAN"

Old poet, I've come to know you only lately,
when in the middle of the road of life,
I now hear time, grown sad,
slipping away, heartbeat by heartbeat.

Your perfume reaches me,
so far from the lands and gardens
that your wandering heart roamed over.
I might have met you in a muted
alley of Toledo, twisting gloomily
down to the river, I might have offered you
a lemon from a patio in Sevilla, a branch
of olives from Lucena, joining you
amid the earthen vessels, singing to the sun,
or picturing blood melting into snow
on Granada's peaks at sunset.

Today your roving fragrance, your exiled
spirit seek me out, pilgrim
of the seas, high, happy,
crazy with amazement at the thunder,
sailor of God, swept away
by a chariot of waves on fire.

Like you, I feel in my own day
the mysterious call, the wind's
invitation to a voyage from the West,
my heart rigged and ready, my wings
weighed down by night now opening...to the sea,
let me put out to sea, with a course set for morning.

Tú seguías, cantando, tu estrella, yo cantando
sigo mi estrella todavía, mientras
de entre mis manos oigo resbalarse,
latido por latido, duro el tiempo.

Tu poderoso aroma que hoy me llega,
fuerte de siglos y de fe, me empuje,
fijos los ojos, sin temblor y puro,
Yehuda Halevi, poeta, el castellano.

Singing, you followed your star; I'm singing
too, still chasing mine, although
I now hear time, grown hard,
slipping away, heartbeat by heartbeat.

Your powerful perfume reaches me today, redolent
of centuries, of faith, urging me to mirror you,
eyes straight ahead, no trembling, heart pure,
Yehuda Halevi, "The Castilian", poet.

RETORNOS DE LA DULCE LIBERTAD

Podías, cuando fuiste marinero en tierra,
ser más libre que ahora,
yéndote alegremente,
desde las amarradas comarcas encendidas
de tu recién nacido soñar, por los profundos
valles de huertos submarinos, por las verdes
laderas de delfines, sumergidos senderos
que iban a dar a dulces sirenas deseadas.

Podías, bien podías entonces, bien podías,
sin lágrimas inútiles, sin impuestas congojas,
viajar, llenos de viento los labios, con un golpe
de abierta luz en medio del corazón, bien alta
la valerosa vida cayendo de tu frente.
¿En dónde las fronteras entonces, ese miedo,
ese horror a los límites,
ese cerco que escuchas avanzar en la noche
como un triste mandato que ha de cumplirse al alba?

Libertad, dulce mía,
por muy niña que fueses,
por más chicos que fueran tus tiernos pasos, dime,
contéstame si aún tus pequeños oídos
me conocen: ¿No intentas, fugitiva y cantando,
retornarme a tus libres comarcas venturosas?

¿Quién te encarcela, dime? Di, ¿quién te pone grillos?
¿Quién te esposa las alas y quién, dime, cerrojos
clava en tu lengua y sombras pone sólo en tus ámbitos?

RETURN OF SWEET FREEDOM

You could be freer back then,
when you were a sailor on land,
voyaging off happily
from the confined places set aflame
by your new dream, through the deep
valleys of undersea orchards, across the green
slopes of the dolphins, down submerged pathways
that led to the mermaids of myth.

Back then you could go anywhere—not yet
bound by grief, weighed down with useless tears—
your lips full of winds, wide-open
light striking your heart, heroism's
imprint on your brow.
Where were the borders back then, this
fear, this despair over limits,
this siege advancing in the night like
a sad order that must be carried out at dawn?

Freedom, sweet freedom,
however far away you are, however
faint your soft steps now,
answer me if you can still hear me:
runaway, singer, why won't you
take me back to your blessed places?

Who's imprisoning you, tell me? Who has you in chains?
Who's tied back your wings, driven spikes through your tongue?
Who's filled all your spaces with shadows?

Libertad, no me dejes. Vuelve a mí, dura y dulce,
como fresca muchacha madurada en la pena.
Hoy mi brazo es más fuerte que el de ayer, y mi canto,
encendido en el tuyo, puede abrir para siempre,
sobre los horizontes del mar, nuestra mañana.

O freedom, don't leave me for good. Come back to me, still sweet
but toughened, like a young woman ripened by pain.
Today my arm is stronger than before, and my song,
ablaze with yours, can light up a new morning
over the horizon of the sea.

RETORNOS DE NIEBLA EN UN DÍA DE SOL

I

Perros, dementes míos, dulces y hermanos, perros,
párvulos imposibles de tontos y aplicados.
Hoy no eres tú, Centella, andaluza y atlántica,
del colegio y las horas, hurtadas a la Física
o al Latín, en las dunas frente al mar y las piedras
de los castillos. Hoy
no eres tampoco tú, Yemi, la enceguecida
de lagartos feroces entre los biselados
de la sal, ni tampoco
aquel Jazmín angélico, ni Tusca misteriosa,
ni Muki ni esos perros
que desconozco aún pero sé que me buscan
sabiendo que en la casa del buen poeta siempre
hay un mantel y un plato junto a un vaso de agua.

Bajo este sol me irrumpe, como recién urdida
por la punta fulmínea de un rayo, la más bella,
la más valiente y grácil, lineal y armoniosa,
la que llenó mis días peligrosos
y las cuevas sin sueño de mis noches terribles
con el inmenso aroma de su flor plateada.

Vienes herida, Niebla, de escombros y de hambre,
como un pobre soldado perdido que anduviera
anhelando en sus ojos preguntar si la muerte
fue leal con sus otros compañeros.
Déjame que te limpie la sangre en estos bosques
y te lleve despacio a ver el mar tranquilo.

RETURN OF NIEBLA ON A SUNLIT DAY

I

All my crazy dogs, my sweet brothers,
impossibly, both careless and intent, innocent.
It's not you today, Centella—Andalusian, Atlantic,
friend of schoolday hours filched from Physics
or Latin, and given to the dunes facing the sea,
to the stones of the castles. Today
it's not you either, Yemi, dazzled
by wild lizards in the bevellings
of salt, nor that
angelic Jazmín, nor mysterious Tusca,
nor Muki, nor any of those dogs
I've not yet met, but who are looking for me, knowing
that in the house of the good poet, there is always
a dish on the mat and a bowl full of water.

Beneath this sun, there rushes back to me, brought alive
by the sparking tip of a ray, the most beautiful of all,
the most valiant and graceful, clean-limbed and harmonious,
the one who filled my dangerous days
and the sleepless caves of my terrible nights
with the immense perfume of her silvery flower.

Niebla, you come wounded from the rubble, hurt
by hunger, like a poor lost soldier longing
with his eyes to ask if death
was true to all the rest of his companions.
Let me clean off your blood here in the clearing,
let me carry you to where you can see the sea.

II

Éste es el mar que acaso tú no tuviste tiempo
de comprender. Ahora
míralo, Niebla, y húndete
en el innumerable azul de su hermosura.
Levanta tus orejas llovidas como hojas
y escucha lo que quiero con amor responderte.

III

Habrás pensado, Niebla,
que te dejé olvidada
por aquellas bahías y pueblos desventrados.
Que quise que la muerte
con sus negros retumbos
fuera la imagen última
que guardaran tus ojos solitarios al irme.
Habrás pensado, Niebla,
que me fui sin quedarme,
sin que mi corazón corriera desolado
con las puertas abiertas,
tundidas por el viento,
repitiéndote a gritos:
—Ésta es tu casa, Niebla,
tus paredes de siempre,
el hogar que elegiste en una noche helada
para hacerlo más dulce, más de flor, más de sueño.
Habrás pensado, Niebla,
que España se moría

II

This is the sea you probably never
had the time to comprehend. Now
gaze at it, Niebla, and plunge
into its beauty, its innumerable blues.
Then lift your ears, dripping like leaves,
and listen to what my love would have me say.

III

You must have thought, Niebla,
that I left you forgotten,
along with those bays and disembowelled towns.
That I wanted death
with its black thunder
to be the final image in your eyes
after I fled.
You must have thought, Niebla,
that I went away without remaining,
without my heart having been
desolated, its doors
left open, banging in the wind,
crying out to you repeatedly:
This is your home, Niebla,
these walls are yours forever,
the hearth you chose one frozen night
to make it sweeter, more like a flower, or a dream.
You must have thought, Niebla,
that Spain was dying

con mi desesperado, corporal abandono,
invadiendo un nocturno funeral, un silencio
definitivo todo lo que su ayer de sombras
y de heroicos relámpagos
fue creando su día,
su anhelante manaña.
Habrás pensado, Niebla,
lejos ya de tus mares,
sin ti, ya en otros tristes y extranjeros kilómetros,
ignorando en qué prados,
en qué montes u orillas,
yacías pobremente llorando por mi vuelta;
habrás pensado, amarga flor mía, habrás pensado,
y con cuánta dolida razón, que mi memoria
te perdía, cayéndose
tu nombre fiel, tu puro
amor con la caricia de otros nuevos amigos.

Pero no, que aquí estás jubilosa a mi lado,
Niebla de sol y bosques,
viva en mí para siempre,
junto a la mar tranquila.

after my desperate, physical abandonment,
after a funereal darkness, a final silence
invaded her as she was rising from a past
of shadows and heroic lightning flashes
to fashion a new day,
her longed-for future.
You must have thought, Niebla, that
now far from your own seas,
without you, in a sad and foreign land,
not knowing in what meadows,
on what mountainsides or shores,
you lay in misery, weeping for my return,
you must have thought, my bitter flower, and
with what understandable hurt, that my memory
let go of you, allowing your faithful
name, your pure love
to fade away with the touch of newer friends.

But no. For here you are, jubilant at my side,
Niebla of the forests and the sunlight,
alive in me forever
beside the quiet sea.

RETORNOS FRENTE A LOS LITORALES ESPAÑOLES

(Desde el "Florida")

Madre hermosa, tan triste y alegre ayer, me muestras
hoy tu rostro arrugado en la mañana
en que paso ante ti sin poder todavía,
después de tanto tiempo, ni abrazarte.
Sales de las estrellas de la noche
mediterránea, el ceño de neblina,
fuerte, amarrada, grande y dolorosa.
Se ve la nieve en tus cabellos altos
de Granada, teñidos para siempre
de aquella sangre pura que acunaste
y te cantaba —¡ay sierras!— tan dichosa.
No quiero separarte de mis ojos,
de mi corazón, madre, ni un momento
mientras te asomas, lejos, a mirarme.
Te doy vela segura, te custodio
sobre las olas lentas de este barco,
de este balcón que pasa y que me lleva
tan distante otra vez de tu amor, madre mía.
Éste es mi mar, el sueño de mi infancia
de arenas, de delfines y gaviotas.
Salen tus pueblos escondidos, rompen
de tus dulces cortezas litorales,
blancas de cal las frentes, chorreados
de heridas y de sombras de tus héroes.
Por aquí la alegría corrió con el espanto.
Por ese largo y duro

RETURN OF THE SPANISH COASTLINE

(from the "Florida")

My beautiful mother, so sad, yet happy once,
today you show your wrinkled face to me
as I pass right in front of you still powerless
to embrace you, even after so much time.
You rise against the paling stars
of the Mediterranean night, banded by mist,
powerful, enchained, great, suffused with pain.
I see the snow in your high hair:
Granada, stained forever with his blood;
you rocked his cradle and he sang to you
—ay Sierras!—in his joy.
I just can't let you slip out of my eyes,
out of my heart, not even for a moment as
you loom up in the distance and look back at me.
I stand vigil, watching over you
across the slow waves from the deck
of this ship that is passing and will carry me
one more time so far off from your love.
This is my sea, my childhood dream
of sand, seagulls, and dolphins.
Your people break from hiding and escape, tearing
your sweet coastal skin,
your brow whitewashed with lime now dark
with wounds and with the shadows of your heroes.
Here happiness was overrun with terror.
Along that long, steep side

costado que sumerges en la espuma,
fue el calvario de Málaga a Almería,
el despiadado crimen,
todavía —¡oh vergüenza!— sin castigo.
Quisiera me miraras pasar hoy jubiloso
lo mismo que hace tiempo
era dentro de ti,
colegial o soldado,
voz de tu pueblo, canto ardiente y libre
de tus ensangrentadas,
verdes y altas coronas conmovidas.
Dime adiós, madre, como yo te digo,
sin decírtelo casi, adiós, que ahora,
ya otra vez sólo mar y cielo solos,
puedo vivir de nuevo, si lo mandas,
morir, morir también, si así lo quieres.

plunging down into the foam,
the suffering ran from Málaga
to Almería, the ruthless crime
still—for shame!—unpunished.
I wish that you could see me pass by now
as joyful as I was
when I lived inside of you,
schoolboy or soldier, voice
of your people, singing passionate
and free, of your bloodstained
high, green crowns, still quivering.
Say goodbye as I do mother, almost
without saying it goodbye now that once more
already, only sea and sky are left, alone.
I could live again if you command me to,
or die, I'll die, if that is what you want.

RETORNOS DE UN POETA ASESINADO

Has vuelto a mí más viejo y triste en la dormida
luz de un sueño tranquilo de marzo, polvorientas
de un gris inesperado las sienes, y aquel bronce
de olivo que tu mágica juventud sostenía,
surcado por el signo de los años, lo mismo
que si la vida aquella que en vida no tuviste
la hubieras paso a paso ya vivido en la muerte.

Yo no sé qué has querido decirme en esta noche
con tu desprevenida visita, el fino traje
de alpaca luminosa, como recién cortado,
la corbata amarilla y el sufrido cabello
al aire, igual que entonces
por aquellos jardines de estudiantiles chopos
y calientes adelfas.

Tal vez hayas pensado—quiero explicarme ahora
ya en las claras afueras del sueño—que debías
llegar primero a mí desde esas subterráneas
raíces o escondidos manantiales en donde
desesperadamente penan tus huesos.
                                    Dime,
confiésame, confiésame
si en el abrazo mudo que me has dado, en el tierno
ademán de ofrecerme una silla, en la simple
manera de sentarte junto a mí, de mirarme,
sonreír y en silencio, sin ninguna palabra,

RETURN OF AN ASSASSINATED POET

You've come back to me older and sadder in the somnolent
light of a quiet dream in March, your temples
dusted with an unexpected grey, and that bronzed
olive skin that glowed with your magical youth
furrowed by the marks of age, as if
you had lived out day by day in death
the years you never had in life.

I don't know what you wanted to tell me tonight,
appearing out of the blue in a well-cut suit
of glossy alpaca, new-tailored,
with your yellow tie and long-suffering hair
wind-tousled, just like before
in those gardens of student poplars
and summer oleanders.

Perhaps you thought—I want to try to grasp this
now in the clear after-light of the dream—that you ought
to come to me first from those underground
roots or hidden springs where
your bones mourn in despair.
                                        Tell me,
confess to me, say
if by the mute embrace you gave me, by the tender
gesture of offering me a chair, by the simple
act of sitting down beside me, gazing at me,
smiling quietly without a word,

dime si no has querido significar con eso
que, a pesar de las mínimas batallas que reñimos,
sigues unido a mí más que nunca en la muerte
por las veces que acaso
no lo estuvimos—¡ay, perdóname!—en la vida.

Si no es así, retorna nuevamente en el sueño
de otra noche a decírmelo.

tell me if you didn't mean to signify by these
that, despite the little battles that we fought,
you are still joined to me, even more perhaps
in death for all those times—forgive me—
that we failed to be in life.

If this isn't so, come back to me in dream
another night to let me know.

RETORNOS DE LA INVARIABLE POESÍA

¡Oh poesía hermosa, fuerte y dulce,
mi solo mar al fin, que siempre vuelve!
¿Cómo vas a dejarme, cómo un día
pude, ciego, pensar en tu abandono?

Tú eres lo que me queda, lo que tuve,
desde que abrí a la luz, sin comprenderlo.
Fiel en la dicha, fiel en la desgracia,
de tu mano en la paz,
y en el estruendo triste
de la sangre y la guerra, de tu mano.

Yo dormía en las hojas, yo jugaba
por las arenas verdes de los ríos,
subiendo a las veletas de las torres
y a la nevada luna mis trineos.
Y eran tus alas invisibles, era
su soplo grácil quien me conducía.

¿Quién tocó con sus ojos los colores,
quién a las líneas contagió su aire,
y quién, cuando el amor, puso en su flecha
un murmullo de fuentes y palomas?

Luego, el horror, la vida en el espanto,
la juventud ardiendo en sacrificio.
¿Qué sin ti el héroe, qué su pobre muerte
sin el súbito halo de relámpagos
con que tú lo coronas e iluminas?

RETURN OF CONSTANT POETRY

Poetry! Beautiful, strong & sweet, in the end
my only sea. Always, you come back to me.
How would you leave me? How was I
so blind to think you would abandon me?

You are what stays with me. Without understanding it,
I've had you with me since I first opened to light.
True to me in my delight, true in my despair,
taking my hand in peace, and
during the sad & bloody clamor of the war,
taking my hand.

I've slept curled up in petals, I've frolicked
on the green sands by the river,
floated with pennants streaming off the towers,
sledded down slopes up on the snowy moon.
It was your invisible wings conveyed me there,
your breath inside me a transporting wind.

Whose eyes brought out the colors with their touch,
who gave all the lines their melody,
and when love came, who was it tipped his arrow
with a murmuring of fountains & doves?

Then, horror, years of fear,
the young burned up in sacrifice.
What would the hero's death be without you, without
the sudden halo of lightning-flashes
with which you illuminate and crown it?

¡Oh hermana de verdad, oh compañera,
conmigo, desterrada,
conmigo, golpeado y alabado,
conmigo, perseguido;
en la vacilación, firme, segura,
en la firmeza, animadora, alegre,
buena en el odio necesario, buena
y hasta feliz en la melancolía!
¿Qué no voy a esperar de ti en lo que me falte
de júbilo o tormento? ¿Qué no voy
a recibir de ti, di, que no sea
sino para salvarme, alzarme, conferirme?
Me matarán quizás y tú serás mi vida,
viviré más que nunca y no serás mi muerte.
Porque por ti yo he sido, yo soy música,
ritmo veloz, cadencia lenta, brisa
de los juncos, vocablo de la mar, estribillo
de las simples cigarras populares.
Porque por ti soy tú y seré por ti sólo
lo que fuiste y serás para siempre en el tiempo.

My true sister, o compañera,
with me in exile,
with me, praised or shouted down,
with me, hounded;
in my hesitation, steady, firm,
in my steadiness, lively & inspired,
sane when I had to hate, sane
in my melancholy—even cheerful!
With you, what can't I hope for
from future joys & torments?
What will I receive except
what saves me, raises me, is the gift I need?
Maybe they will kill me, and you'll be my only life:
I'll be more alive than ever; I won't die because of you.
Because through you I'm one with music, I'm
swift rhythm & slow cadence, a breeze
through the rushes, syllables from the sea,
the refrain of the simple cicadas.
Because I have become you, and will only be
what you've been and will always be through time.

RETORNOS DEL PUEBLO ESPAÑOL

En verdad, tú no tienes
que retornar a mí, porque siempre has estado
y estás en la corriente continua de mi sangre.
Pero a veces hay días y nocturnos momentos
sobre todo en que el cauce de las venas se agranda
y subes a la cima del corazón y entonces
arrojándote afuera
me iluminas y envuelves arrastrándome.

¡Qué claro que me pareces así, cómo te veo
de ese modo a mi lado, cómo tu combatida
sombra se hace de luz, y es tu mar, son los círculos
de tus ilimitadas ondas los que me llevan
fundido y confundido con tu ser, con tu antigua
leyenda, con tus verdes y misteriosos mitos,
tu verídica historia pasada y real presente!

Te conocí en las plazas, primero, y por las calles
marineras. Girando,
mi corazón, en ronda, bajaba entretejido
al de tus claros juegos y canciones.

> *¡Ay, niña!*
> *La sirenita del mar*
> *es una pulida dama*
> *es una dama pulida.*
> *¡Ay, niña!*
> *Que por una maldición*
> *vive perdida en el agua,*
> *vive en el agua perdida.*
> *¡Ay, niña!*

'

RETURN OF THE SPANISH PEOPLE

Actually, you don't need to return to me.
You are and always have been deep
within the current of my blood.
But sometimes it's as if the channel
is too narrow, and you rise up to the top
of my heart and burst out, a force
outside me now,
casting light, and urging me along.

Yes, this is just how I see you: at my side.
Even your shadow is combative,
although it's made of light. And now
I'm remembering your sea, borne along
by your limitless waves, I am fused
and confused with your being, your ancient
legend, your green and mysterious myths.

I came to know you first in the plazas,
in the sea-wending streets. And my heart
went spinning around, awhirl
with your games and your songs.

Girls! Watch out!
The little mermaid in the sea
was a lady once,
fine as could be.
Girls! Watch out!
Because of a curse
she was suddenly worse:
she's lost in the water, she lives in the sea.
Girls! Watch out!

No sólo fue mi mano la tuya desde entonces,
sino que todo yo fui ya tú: tu garganta,
la cuna, desde entonces, de mi lengua;
tus ojos, desde entonces, los míos, igualmente
para el llanto profundo o fluvial alegría;
tus bellas explosiones, tu creadora hambre,
toda tu caudalosa fortaleza,
ese toro que escondes y lanzas de improviso.

> *Ya se van los segadores*
> (Pronto, un día, volverán.)
> *a segar en el secano,*
> (Pronto, un día, volverán.)
> *a beber agua de balsa,*
> (Pronto, un día, volverán.)
> *toda llena de gusanos.*
> (Pronto, un día, volverán,
> con la luz entre las manos.)

Luego, cuando a torrente te alzaste, cuando a cimas,
cuando en mortal centella descendiste, batiendo
la ensangrentada oscuridad, el crimen
de tenebrosos, turbios, deformados
de la traición, del robo
de tu encendido despertar, entonces,
cuando aquella inicial de victorioso acero,
subí contigo a vértice, a arrebolada cumbre
de laurel, derramándome
de tu palpitación,
de tu estado de gracia incontenible,
tu claridad sencilla cantando ante la muerte.

Not only was my hand yours from then on,
but all of me turned into you: your throat
was now the cradle of my tongue;
my eyes were now your eyes, they wept
with your laments, filled with your joy;
I lived your beautiful explosions, felt your
creative hunger and abundant strength, I knew
that bull you hide and then release out of the blue.

> *Now the reapers all have gone*
> (One day, soon, they will return.)
> *to harvest dried-up, sunburned lands,*
> (One day, soon, they will return.)
> *they drink their water from stale ponds,*
> (One day, soon, they will return.)
> *and every sip contains a worm.*
> (One day, soon, they will return,
> holding light between their hands.)

Later, you breasted the torrent, you climbed to the summit,
descending like a mortal flash of lightning, beating back
the bloodied darkness, the crime
of those shadowy, distorted figures:
treason, and the theft
of our new-kindled awakening. Then,
after the first winning clashes of steel,
I rose with you, sharing your crown of red clouds,
of laurel, feeling flow into me not just
your pounding breath, but
your state of grace, your simple
clarity, singing in the face of death.

Ya vienen los invasores
(Corazón, corazón, que te hieren.)
por montes, mares y llanos.
(Corazón, corazón, que te matan.)
Son alemanes y moros,
(¡A cantar, corazón, si me dejas!)
portugueses e italianos.
(¡A cantar, corazón, si me acabas!)
Y por los campos de España
(Corazón, corazón, no te hieren.)
mueren parientes y hermanos.
(Corazón, corazón, no te matan.)

Después, las sombras del nocturno triste,
la ayudada victoria del helado enemigo,
de esos hierros mortales, pobre pueblo, que siempre
igual que una cintura invisible te esperan.
Y cuando rebosaste los muros, los agónicos
pozos de las prisiones, los campos de trabajo
en donde traspiraste por la boca hasta el alma,
aún me llegó de ti, sobre el mar, ese viento,
ese sostén de piedra que hoy a tantos kilómetros
asegura las alas iguales de mi canto.

Me hirieron, me golpearon
(Tomo ejemplo y miro en ti.)
y aunque me dieron la muerte
(Tomo ejemplo y miro en ti.)
nunca jamás me doblaron.
(Tomo ejemplo y miro en ti.
Tus hombros me acompañaron.)

Now come the invaders
(O heart, they're hurting you.)
across mountains, seas, and plains.
(O heart, they're killing you.)
Germans come and Moors,
(I'll sing, heart, if you'll let me!)
Portuguese and Italians.
(A song, heart, if you'll finish it!)
And over the fields of Spain,
(O heart, they cannot hurt you.)
kinsmen and brothers are dying.
(O heart, they cannot kill you.)

Afterward, shadows of night-sorrow,
the much-assisted triumph of the enemy and
his mortal weapons, o my people, always
one more lash of the invisible belt.
And when you overflowed the cells, the killing
pits of the prisons, the fields of forced labor
where you sighed from your mouth down to your soul,
you still managed to send to me, across the sea,
that strong sustaining wind, which even from so far
buoys up the wings of my unchanging song.

They wounded me, they struck me
(You gave me your example.)
they ordered up my death
(You gave me your example.)
but I never did give way.
(You gave me your example.
Your shoulders bore my burden.)

Y así es, así eres en tu hermandad, lo mismo
que en tus claros e insomnes sufrimientos. Que nunca
tu valor, el amor alegre que me diste,
la dignidad austera que entraste en mi garganta,
esos años de luz con los que todavía
haces resplandecer de juventud mi frente,
se oscurezcan en mí, sino que pronto puedan,
ceñidos a tu sangre de nuevo, correr juntos
y con la misma voz celebrar levantados
el ya definitivo subir de nuestro día.

This is your humanity, manifested
even through your endless suffering.
Your courage, the joyous love you gave me,
the austere dignity you once lent to my voice,
those years of light—my youth with you—
that still shine in my face—may these not
grow dim in me, but may my blood
always flow in unison with yours, and may
we soon lift up one voice to celebrate
the definitive re-dawning of our day.

NOTES ON THE POEMS

"Returning on a Birthday (J.R.J.)": J.R.J. is the great Spanish poet Juan Ramón Jiménez, who belonged to the generation before Alberti, the "Generation of '98". Here, Alberti remembers taking his first poems to Juan Ramón. With the exception of "Returning to Chopin, Brought to Life by Hands Now Gone", which imitates certain études and nocturnes by Chopin and even contains a refrain, and "Return of the Spanish People", into which Alberti weaves pieces of Andalucían songs, "Birthday" is the only poem in the book whose form differs from *Returnings'* norm. The very short lines here are meant to evoke the song-poems which were Alberti's first writings, thus giving us an idea of the poems he brought that day to the older poet.

"Return of Yehuda Halevi, 'The Castilian'": Yehuda Halevi was a Spanish medieval (1075-1141) Jewish poet whose work Alberti discovered in exile, finding inspiration in Halevi's determination to return to the Jewish Homeland.

"Return of Niebla on a Sunlit Day": Niebla ("mist") was the orphaned dog rescued one misty night by Alberti and his friend Pablo Neruda after a bombing raid. Niebla became Alberti's constant, enheartening companion during the war, accompanying him on his dangerous drives into the mountains to hide the Prado's paintings, and even going with him to the front. Sadly, Alberti was forced to abandon Niebla on the day he fled Spain, there being no room for her on the single-engine plane. He never got over this. The following is my translation of the formal 20-line poem Alberti wrote for Niebla during the war:

TO MY DOG NIEBLA

> It's what your ears sing, though beyond your mind;
> it's in your foolish, innocent look, and in the shine
> you leave across the mountain when you bound:
> sweet streak, Niebla, coil of light unwound.

These days, so many tentative, orphaned dogs,
appearing amid clearings in the fog,
disoriented, dragging with their trouble:
the recent terror of their homes in rubble.

Despite the lack of ceremonial trains—instead
vans flee with their bare boxes full of dead;
the boys who now watch battles in the air
as if they were the fireworks of some fair;

despite the loss of my best friend;
my family, who do not comprehend
precisely what I care the most about;
despite the one who left and sold us out;

Niebla, comrade of mine,
through this heroic, bombed-out, painful time,
there remains for us what they cannot destroy:
the faith we share in joy, in joy, in joy.

"Return of an Assassinated Poet": Here the poet evokes Federico García Lorca. Alberti and Lorca were very close friends, but also poetic rivals. The rivalry was sometimes intense, and there may have been a slight rift which needed to be healed when the poets parted for the summer in 1936; each thought the parting was temporary, but Lorca was murdered by the Fascists while Alberti was still trapped on Ibiza, so they never saw each other again. In the poem, a dream brings them together once more.

The Translator

Carolyn L. Tipton is a poet, translator, and teacher in the Fall Program for Freshmen at the University of California, Berkeley. Her awards include fellowships from the National Endowment for the Humanities and the National Endowment for the Arts. Her translation of *To Painting: Poems by Rafael Alberti*, won the National Translation Award.